The Spanish Civil War: A Very Short Introduction

'This is far and away the best short introduction to the Spanish Civil War that I have read in any language.'
Professor Paul Preston, London School of Economics

VERY SHORT INTRODUCTIONS are for anyone wanting a stimulating and accessible way in to a new subject. They are written by experts, and have been published in more than 25 languages worldwide.

The series began in 1995, and now represents a wide variety of topics in history, philosophy, religion, science, and the humanities. Over the next few years it will grow to a library of around 200 volumes – a Very Short Introduction to everything from ancient Egypt and Indian philosophy to conceptual art and cosmology.

Very Short Introductions available now:

ANARCHISM   Colin Ward
ANCIENT EGYPT   Ian Shaw
ANCIENT PHILOSOPHY
   Julia Annas
ANCIENT WARFARE
   Harry Sidebottom
THE ANGLO-SAXON AGE
   John Blair
ANIMAL RIGHTS
   David DeGrazia
ARCHAEOLOGY   Paul Bahn
ARCHITECTURE
   Andrew Ballantyne
ARISTOTLE   Jonathan Barnes
ART HISTORY   Dana Arnold
ART THEORY   Cynthia Freeland
THE HISTORY OF
   ASTRONOMY   Michael Hoskin
ATHEISM   Julian Baggini
AUGUSTINE   Henry Chadwick
BARTHES   Jonathan Culler
THE BIBLE   John Riches
BRITISH POLITICS
   Anthony Wright
BUDDHA   Michael Carrithers
BUDDHISM   Damien Keown
CAPITALISM   James Fulcher
THE CELTS   Barry Cunliffe
CHOICE THEORY
   Michael Allingham
CHRISTIAN ART   Beth Williamson

CHRISTIANITY   Linda Woodhead
CLASSICS   Mary Beard and
   John Henderson
CLAUSEWITZ   Michael Howard
THE COLD WAR   Robert McMahon
CONSCIOUSNESS   Sue Blackmore
CONTINENTAL PHILOSOPHY
   Simon Critchley
COSMOLOGY   Peter Coles
CRYPTOGRAPHY
   Fred Piper and Sean Murphy
DADA AND SURREALISM
   David Hopkins
DARWIN   Jonathan Howard
DEMOCRACY   Bernard Crick
DESCARTES   Tom Sorell
DRUGS   Leslie Iversen
THE EARTH   Martin Redfern
EGYPTIAN MYTH   Geraldine Pinch
EIGHTEENTH-CENTURY
   BRITAIN   Paul Langford
EMOTION   Dylan Evans
EMPIRE   Stephen Howe
ENGELS   Terrell Carver
ETHICS   Simon Blackburn
THE EUROPEAN UNION
   John Pinder
EVOLUTION
   Brian and Deborah Charlesworth
FASCISM   Kevin Passmore
FOUCAULT   Gary Gutting

THE FRENCH REVOLUTION
  William Doyle
FREE WILL   Thomas Pink
FREUD   Anthony Storr
GALILEO   Stillman Drake
GANDHI   Bhikhu Parekh
GLOBALIZATION   Manfred Steger
GLOBAL WARMING   Mark Maslin
HEGEL   Peter Singer
HEIDEGGER   Michael Inwood
HIEROGLYPHS   Penelope Wilson
HINDUISM   Kim Knott
HISTORY   John H. Arnold
HOBBES   Richard Tuck
HUME   A. J. Ayer
IDEOLOGY   Michael Freeden
INDIAN PHILOSOPHY
  Sue Hamilton
INTELLIGENCE   Ian J. Deary
ISLAM   Malise Ruthven
JUDAISM   Norman Solomon
JUNG   Anthony Stevens
KAFKA   Ritchie Robertson
KANT   Roger Scruton
KIERKEGAARD   Patrick Gardiner
THE KORAN   Michael Cook
LINGUISTICS   Peter Matthews
LITERARY THEORY
  Jonathan Culler
LOCKE   John Dunn
LOGIC   Graham Priest
MACHIAVELLI   Quentin Skinner
MARX   Peter Singer
MATHEMATICS
  Timothy Gowers
MEDICAL ETHICS   Tony Hope
MEDIEVAL BRITAIN
  John Gillingham and Ralph A. Griffiths
MODERN ART   David Cottington
MODERN IRELAND   Senia Pašeta
MOLECULES   Philip Ball
MUSIC   Nicholas Cook
MYTH   Robert A. Segal

NIETZSCHE   Michael Tanner
NINETEENTH-CENTURY
  BRITAIN   Christopher Harvie and
  H. C. G. Matthew
NORTHERN IRELAND
  Marc Mulholland
PARTICLE PHYSICS
  Frank Close
PAUL   E. P. Sanders
PHILOSOPHY   Edward Craig
PHILOSOPHY OF SCIENCE
  Samir Okasha
PLATO   Julia Annas
POLITICS   Kenneth Minogue
POLITICAL PHILOSOPHY
  David Miller
POSTCOLONIALISM
  Robert Young
POSTMODERNISM
  Christopher Butler
POSTSTRUCTURALISM
  Catherine Belsey
PREHISTORY   Chris Gosden
PRESOCRATIC PHILOSOPHY
  Catherine Osborne
PSYCHOLOGY   Gillian Butler and
  Freda McManus
QUANTUM THEORY
  John Polkinghorne
ROMAN BRITAIN
  Peter Salway
ROUSSEAU   Robert Wokler
RUSSELL   A. C. Grayling
RUSSIAN LITERATURE
  Catriona Kelly
THE RUSSIAN REVOLUTION
  S. A. Smith
SCHIZOPHRENIA
  Chris Frith and Eve Johnstone
SCHOPENHAUER
  Christopher Janaway
SHAKESPEARE
  Germaine Greer

SOCIAL AND CULTURAL
  ANTHROPOLOGY
  John Monaghan and Peter Just
SOCIOLOGY   Steve Bruce
SOCRATES   C. C. W. Taylor
THE SPANISH CIVIL WAR
  Helen Graham
SPINOZA   Roger Scruton

STUART BRITAIN   John Morrill
TERRORISM   Charles Townshend
THEOLOGY   David F. Ford
THE TUDORS   John Guy
TWENTIETH-CENTURY
  BRITAIN   Kenneth O. Morgan
WITTGENSTEIN   A. C. Grayling
WORLD MUSIC   Philip Bohlman

Available soon:

AFRICAN HISTORY
  John Parker and Richard Rathbone
THE BRAIN   Michael O'Shea
BUDDHIST ETHICS
  Damien Keown
CHAOS   Leonard Smith
CITIZENSHIP   Richard Bellamy
CLASSICAL ARCHITECTURE
  Robert Tavernor
CONTEMPORARY ART
  Julian Stallabrass
THE CRUSADES
  Christopher Tyerman
DERRIDA   Simon Glendinning
DESIGN   John Heskett
DINOSAURS   David Norman
DREAMING   J. Allan Hobson
ECONOMICS   Partha Dasgupta
THE ELEMENTS   Philip Ball
THE END OF THE WORLD
  Bill McGuire
EXISTENTIALISM   Thomas Flynn
FEMINISM   Margaret Walters
THE FIRST WORLD WAR
  Michael Howard
FUNDAMENTALISM
  Malise Ruthven
HABERMAS   Gordon Finlayson
HUMAN EVOLUTION
  Bernard Wood

INTERNATIONAL RELATIONS
  Paul Wilkinson
JAZZ   Brian Morton
MANDELA   Tom Lodge
THE MARQUIS DE SADE
  John Phillips
THE MIND   Martin Davies
NATIONALISM   Steven Grosby
PERCEPTION   Richard Gregory
PHILOSOPHY OF RELIGION
  Jack Copeland and Diane Proudfoot
PHOTOGRAPHY   Steve Edwards
THE RAJ   Denis Judd
RACISM   Ali Rattansi
THE RENAISSANCE
  Jerry Brotton
RENAISSANCE ART
  Geraldine Johnson
ROMAN EMPIRE
  Christopher Kelly
SARTRE   Christina Howells
SIKHISM   Eleanor Nesbitt
SOCIALISM   Michael Newman
TIME   Leofranc Holford-Strevens
TRAGEDY   Adrian Poole
THE TWENTIETH CENTURY
  Martin Conway
THE WORLD TRADE
  ORGANIZATION
  Amrita Narlikar

For more information visit our web site
www.oup.co.uk/vsi/

Helen Graham

THE SPANISH
CIVIL WAR

A Very Short Introduction

OXFORD
UNIVERSITY PRESS

OXFORD

UNIVERSITY PRESS

Great Clarendon Street, Oxford OX2 6DP

Oxford University Press is a department of the University of Oxford.
It furthers the University's objective of excellence in research, scholarship,
and education by publishing worldwide in

Oxford New York

Auckland Cape Town Dar es Salaam Hong Kong Karachi Kuala Lumpur
Madrid Melbourne Mexico City Nairobi New Delhi Shanghai Taipei Toronto

With offices in

Argentina Austria Brazil Chile Czech Republic France Greece
Guatemala Hungary Italy Japan South Korea Poland Portugal
Singapore Switzerland Thailand Turkey Ukraine Vietnam

Oxford is a registered trade mark of Oxford University Press
in the UK and in certain other countries

Published in the United States
by Oxford University Press Inc., New York

British Library Cataloguing in Publication Data

Data available

Library of Congress Cataloging-in-Publication Data

Graham, Helen.
The Spanish Civil War : a very short introduction / Helen Graham.
p. cm. — (Very short introductions)
Includes bibliographical references and index.
1. Spain—History—Civil War, 1936–1939.   I. Title.   II. Series.
DP269.G6462 2005
946.081—dc22   2004029461

ISBN 13: 978-0-19-280377-1

ISBN 10: 0-19-280377-8

3 5 7 9 10 8 6 4 2

Typeset by RefineCatch Ltd, Bungay, Suffolk
Printed in Great Britain by
Ashford Colour Press Ltd, Gosport, Hants

You must remember this and see that others remember.

(Luis Cernuda)

The greatest challenge of the new millennium is not to mythologize our fears.

Contents

Preface and acknowledgements   ix

List of maps and illustrations   xiii

1   The origins of Spain's civil war   1

2   Rebellion, revolution, and repression   21

3   Mobilize and survive: the Republic at war   37

4   The making of rebel Spain   68

5   The Republic besieged   87

6   Victory and defeat: the wars after the war   115

7   The uses of history   138

References   151

Further reading   154

Chronology   159

Glossary   167

Index   169

Preface and acknowledgements

Amid the wrenching catastrophes of 20th-century European history, the Spanish Civil War continues today to exert a particular fascination. Certainly this force of attraction cannot be explained in terms of the geographical or human scale of the conflict or the technological horrors it witnessed. For the Spanish strife is dwarfed by other conflicts – in terms of material destruction and human tragedy. This is true even if we include in our calculations the continuing horror of mass killing and incarceration that was the 'post-war' in 1940s Spain. But our enduring engagement with the Spanish Civil War is undeniable. It has generated over fifteen thousand books – a textual epitaph that puts it on a par with the Second World War.

The main purpose of this short book is to explain the Civil War – its causes, course, and consequences, in both a domestic and international context. It does not deal in any detail with battles or strategy, so readers seeking conventional military history should look elsewhere (see further reading). But it is concerned throughout with how war affected the physical and psychic lives of soldiers and civilians, and how it shaped the course of politics, society, and culture inside Spain but also beyond.

The Spanish Civil War was the first fought in Europe in which civilians became targets *en masse*, through bombing raids on big cities. The new photo-journalism that made Spain's the first 'photogenic' war in history also transmitted searing images of the vast numbers of political refugees produced by the conflict. There had been mass population displacements during the First World War, but none had had Spain's visibility. The Civil War made a deep impression on those watching from other European countries. For Spaniards themselves, the shock was huge. There were no remotely comparative terms of reference for the military, industrial, social, and political mobilization the Civil War produced, since Spain had not participated in the First World War of 1914–18. As is well known, Spain also became the place where other powers tested the latest technologies of warfare. Even more bleakly, the conflict revealed what war on European soil could mean – presaging the purificatory, genocidal, and retributive conflicts of those many other civil wars waged across the continent between 1939 and the end of the 1940s.

What this also indicates is that, even in its origins, the Spanish Civil War was an intrinsically European phenomenon. This is not to suggest that the tensions and anxieties inside Spanish society that led to the war-unleashing military coup were other than domestically generated. But social and political polarization over issues such as mass suffrage, social welfare reform, and the redistribution of land and economic power in the countryside were not specific to Spain; nor were the culture wars being fought (already before the outbreak of the Civil War) over secularizing reform and between cosmopolitan urbanism and rural tradition. The supposed 'solutions' to the Spanish conflict would also bear all the hallmarks of the monolithic recipes imposed elsewhere by other fascist and quasi-fascist regimes in Europe. This shared context offers the key to why the Civil War had such an enormous impact beyond Spain and why a sense of the war's importance continues to resonate today. The second purpose of this book is thus to examine the historical debates and political polemics to which the war has given rise. For arguing about the Civil War has never been the sole province of professional historians – inside Spain or beyond.

Chapter 1 offers a thematic explanation of the conflictual factors in 20th-century Spanish history, exploring the ways they played out in the 1930s. It does not provide a complete chronological narrative of the pre-war Republican years (1931–6) since this is readily available in many other places (see further reading). These conflicts are followed up in Chapter 2, which explores how different social and political constituencies sought to 'resolve' them in the course of the events unleashed by the military coup of 17–18 July 1936. These two opening chapters also sketch the culture of barracks and (colonial) battlefield that produced the army officers who rebelled against the democratic Second Republic. Among them was General Francisco Franco who rose to supreme military and political command during the Civil War, and, having won it, ruled Spain for the next 36 years. Chapters 3, 4, and 5 explore the escalation of the war through the complex process of its internationalization; the ways in which the experience of war shaped politics and society in both Republican and Francoist zones; and how, ultimately, great power politics and diplomacy determined the outcome of the conflict.

Throughout, the book focuses on the Civil War as an arena of social change where different ideas about culture (understood in its broadest sense) were forged or resisted and in which both Spaniards and non-Spaniards participated alike. These were conflicts that would continue elsewhere – in Europe and beyond, also with Spanish participation – during the Second World War of 1939–45. Chapter 6 takes up these themes and also the violent repression enacted inside Spain by a regime that envisaged itself as part of the Nazi new order in Europe. Integral to the totalitarian aspirations of victorious Francoism was an attempt to obliterate the memory of the defeated. History writing itself became a battleground. Chapter 7 charts the regime's attempt to appropriate the past. It also indicates its ultimate failure – as evident in new history writing on the war and, above all, in the return of Republican memory now occurring through the channels of civil society in Spain in the opening years of the 21st century.

The further reading section at the end of the book offers a short list of introductory material in English. I have also included a few more eclectic suggestions, as well as several of the most relevant websites.

However, readers should be aware that much of the most innovative scholarly research on the Spanish Civil War is unavailable in English. The further reading cannot, therefore, give a sense of the range and the richness of the leading-edge bibliography, now predominantly in Spanish, but it will, I hope, provide a useful starting point for the general reader.

Throughout the text I use 'republican(s)' to denote ideologically republican parties and their members. When the term is capitalized ('Republican(s)') it refers to *all* those groups and individuals who supported the Spanish Republic during the Civil War – including socialists, communists, and anarcho-syndicalists. Thus, many 'Republicans' were not specifically 'republican'.

I would like to thank all the people who read drafts of my text, and also Emily Jolliffe and Marsha Filion for being kind and patient editors. For specific help with written or visual sources or technological assistance, I am indebted to (in alphabetical order): Peter Anderson, Richard Baxell, Benito Bermejo, the Campañá family, Hilary Canavan, Cornell Capa, Jane Durán, the late Harry Fisher, Lala Isla, Conxita Mir, Cary Nelson, Paul Preston, Alex Quiroga, Antonina Rodrigo, Francisco Romero, Mariano Sanz, Ramón Sender Barayón, Rémi Skoutelsky, Mary Vincent, and Ricard Vinyes. More generally, I would like to thank my friends, colleagues, and students for everything they have taught me about the collective endeavour of doing history. All remaining shortcomings and errors are, of course, entirely my own responsibility.

List of maps and illustrations

1 The division of Spain,
22 July 1936   20
Copyright Cambridge University
Press

2 Rebel soldiers take
southern town   22
Archivo Serrano, Hemeroteca
Municipal de Sevilla, Spain

3 Amparo Barayón   30
Private collection, courtesy
of Ramón Sender Barayón

4 Oliver Law   45
Private collection, courtesy
of the late Harry Fisher

5 Shop window
iconography   50
Kati Horna collection, Ministry
of Culture, Archivo General de la
Guerra Civil Española, Spain

6 Republican youth
mobilization   54
Private collection, courtesy
of Antonina Rodrigo

7 *Miliciana*   55
Instituto de España, London

8 Republican woman
war worker   56
Ministry of Culture, Archivo
General de la Administración,
Spain

9 Literacy class   56
Biblioteca Nacional, Madrid

10 Republican health
education poster   57
Ministry of Culture,
Archivo General de la
Guerra Civil Española,
Spain

11 Propaganda train   58
Photo: Antoni Campañá,
reproduced courtesy of the
Campañá family

12 Wall poem   59
Courtesy of Cary Nelson

13 Moscow fashion 62
Ministry of Culture,
Archivo General de la Guerra
Civil Española, Spain

14 ¡Kultur! 72
Ministry of Culture, Archivo
General de la Guerra Civil
Española, Spain

15 Women in rebel
zone, war work 77
Biblioteca Nacional, Madrid

16 Women in rebel
zone, saluting the
flag 77
Ministry of Culture, Archivo
General de la Administración,
Spain

17 The division of
Spanish territory,
July 1938 97
Copyright Cambridge
University Press

18 Child street-seller in
Republican zone 106
Kati Horna collection, Ministry
of Culture, Archivo General de la
Guerra Civil Española, Spain

19 Desfile de la Victoria
(Franco's victory
parade) 116
Actualidad Española

20 Republican refugee
camp on French
beach 118
Photo: Robert Capa,
copyright Magnum Photos

21 Red poster 124
Bibliothèque de Documentation
Internationale Contemporaine
(BDIC) et Musée d'Histoire
Contemporaine, Paris

22 Francisco Boix 128
Courtesy of Benito Bermejo

23 Political prisoners 130
Agencia EFE, Madrid

The publisher and the author apologize for any errors or omissions in the above list. If contacted they will be pleased to rectify these at the earliest opportunity.

Chapter 1
The origins of Spain's civil war

Long live those who bring us the rule of law.

The Spanish Civil War began with a military coup. There was a long history of military intervention in Spain's political life. But the coup of 17–18 July 1936 was an old instrument being used for a new purpose. It aimed to halt the mass political democracy set in train by the effects of the First World War and the Russian Revolution, and accelerated by the ensuing social, economic, and cultural changes of the 1920s and 1930s. In this sense, the military rising against Spain's democratic Second Republic was the equivalent of the fascist takeovers that followed the coming to power of Mussolini in Italy (1922) and Hitler in Germany (1933) and which were also designed to control similar manifestations of social, political, and cultural change.

It may at first seem paradoxical that the clash between old and new should have erupted into full-scale civil war in the relative backwater of Spain. First and foremost, however, we need to remember that the escalation from military coup to civil war and then to a modern, 'total' war involving the vast majority of the civilian population, was crucially dependent on factors that were external to the Spanish arena. It is also true that when Spaniards retrospectively attribute the *causes* of the civil war, they often describe thoughts and feelings that were produced *by the war itself*.

Notwithstanding the currency of ideas about 'two Spains' ready to confront each other on 18 July 1936, 'us' and 'them' were categories actively made by the violent experience of the war and did not fully exist prior to it.

Nevertheless, even in the immediate aftermath of the July military coup and before any international factors could come into play, extreme forms of internecine violence were already occurring virtually throughout Spain. So historians are required to explore what this violence meant and how it related to the pre-war domestic environment. Three factors were crucial here. First, the extremely uneven levels of development that obtained inside Spain by the 1930s. This meant that the military coup unleashed what was in effect a series of culture wars: urban culture and cosmopolitan lifestyles versus rural tradition; secular against religious; authoritarianism against liberal political cultures; centre versus periphery; traditional gender roles versus the 'new woman'; even youth against age, since generational conflicts were also present. Second, the force with which the opposing elements clashed owed more than a little to the cultural influence of a manichaean brand of Catholicism that still predominated in Spain, affecting even many of those who had consciously rejected religious belief and the authority of the Church. Third, since the detonator of events was a military coup, we must also examine the role played by Spain's army and, in particular, the emergence of a rigid and intolerant political culture in its officer corps during the early decades of the 20th century.

Crucial to all of these factors, but especially the military, was Spain's final loss of empire in 1898. This deprived the country of its protected external markets and in so doing kick-started an intermittent and acrimonious debate over how Spain should modernize itself economically and who should bear the cost. The arguments in favour of domestic reform made by Spain's relatively more progressive industrial elites, especially those based in the Catalan textile sector, made little headway. They came up against

2

the interests of an entrenched agrarian sector that was inevitably more powerful in a country whose economy was still mainly based in agriculture. The large landowners whose estates dominated the southern half of Spain would have been the elite sector most affected by economic and political reform. Temperamentally too they were inflexible; many were the fathers and elder brothers of Spain's officer elites – groups known for being profoundly suspicious of change.

The loss of empire deprived Spain's over-large officer corps, which had been inherited from the continuous wars of the 19th century, of any meaningful external defensive role. In so doing, imperial defeat turned the military into a powerful internal political lobby determined to find a new role while guarding against any loss of income or prestige in the interim. To take the sting out of defeat, there grew up within the officer corps a powerful myth that civilian politicians had been uniquely responsible for the final loss of empire and thus had little moral claim on governing the country. This belief was already deeply ingrained by the time the 15-year-old Francisco Franco entered the military academy in 1907. A generation of officer cadets came to see themselves as the defenders of Spain's unity and hierarchy and of its cultural and political homogeneity, as consubstantial with the country's historic greatness. Indeed, many in the military elite took this one step further, interpreting their defence of this idea of 'Spain' as a new *imperial* duty – thereby interpreting in reverse the monarchical constitution that defined Spain's colonial territories as provinces of the metropolis. What was deadly about this new interpretation of imperial defence was that it came to be directed against other groups of Spaniards who symbolized the social and economic changes occurring in the towns and cities.

These changes were slower than in some other European countries, but by the second decade of the 20th century urban Spain was on the move. Towns like Seville and Zaragoza grew as industry (albeit on a small scale) expanded beyond the traditional areas of the north (coal mines, iron and steel foundries, shipbuilding) and northeast (Catalan textiles). Similarly affected was the Valencia region on the northeast seaboard, where urbanization and industrial development reinforced an historic anti-centralism (federalism). These economic changes and the developments that accompanied them – such as better communications and transport and the relatively freer circulation of new ideas – created new social constituencies: an urban professional sector and industrial workers, both of whom increasingly wanted a political voice. The traditional order with its highly restrictive franchise was thus coming under increasing strain in urban Spain.

But another country existed that was still far less affected by these demands. This was rural and provincial Spain, *la España profunda*. Most of Spain's 20 million people (21,303,000 in 1920) still lived in villages and small towns. In the centre and north, the bulk of the population were peasant smallholders, most of them of modest means, some very poor. This rural society was serviced by the populations of agrarian or market towns, inhabited by a provincial middle class of similar social attitudes. It was a rigid world bound by the ties of custom and tradition in which a conservative form of Catholicism provided the common language, value, and culture. The close relationship between Church and community in centre-north Spain was cemented by the crucial pastoral role played by local priests. Not only did the Church provide spiritual solace but also practical support – often in the shape of rural credit banks that offered a life-saving resource to an impoverished small peasantry perpetually threatened by crop failure and fearful of falling prey to money lenders. The reciprocal desire of Church and community to protect the other stemmed from a common fear of dull-rumoured change and an identification with an older cherished world of order and hierarchy. Many identified specifically with monarchy as the form of government best able to protect this order. The Church hierarchy clung to it not least to stave off the consequences of encroaching political liberalism and cultural pluralism – both of which profoundly challenged its own monopoly on truth.

For by the early decades of the 20th century, the Catholic Church in Spain already felt itself to be under siege. Not only did it have little authority among urban workers, but the teeming poor of the rural south were also long lost to it. The agricultural labourers of Spain's 'deep south' viewed the Church as a pillar and perpetuator of a landed order that oppressed them. Southern Spain was dominated by massive estates worked by landless peasants whose lives were a constant struggle against starvation. The norm of huge estates growing a single crop meant that labourers were dependent on a sole source of income, which, even then, was only available for part of the year – at planting and harvesting times. In the absence of any public welfare provision or other forms of poor relief, this dependency turned the landless poor into virtual slaves at the disposal of landlords and estate bailiffs. Labourers were brutalized by estate stewards and the rural police, the hated civil guard who shot unemployed workers foraging for acorns and wood on estate land. The fact that the local priest invariably acted as the ally of the landowner and police chief made the rural poor fiercely anticlerical and turned religion in the south into a viciously divisive issue of politics and social class. The systematic abuse of the powerless made violence endemic in this tightly repressed rural society. But the periodic slave revolts of the rural poor were easily repressed by the police – no less after the First World War than in earlier periods.

Nevertheless, in urban Spain the First World War was, as elsewhere in Europe, the crucial detonator of social change. Spain did not participate militarily. But the war produced both an economic boom and also severe forms of inflation and dislocation that drastically affected poorer sectors of society – both rural and urban. It was in urban Spain, however, that the resulting social protest seriously alarmed elite groups, who now viewed indigenous protest through the lens of the Russian Revolution. The epicentre of the threat was 'red' Barcelona. But for the Spanish establishment the spectre was not bolshevism but the city's powerful anarcho-syndicalist trade union movement, the CNT. It was committed to direct and often violent action against intransigent employers who conspired with the military authorities, and even in one notorious case with a high-ranking army officer, who was Barcelona's civil governor, to assassinate leading CNT trade unionists. In order to quell labour unrest in Barcelona and reimpose conservative order across Spain, a 'soft' military coup was made in 1923 by General Miguel Primo de Rivera. It was welcomed by the reigning monarch, King Alfonso XIII, who strongly favoured military over constitutional solutions to the problems of government.

The dictatorship's way was also eased by the economic boom of the 1920s. But at the same time this intensified the demands of urban middle-class sectors for political reform. They wanted constitutional rights as a defence of their own interests against the arbitrary power of the dictator. Political parties were illegal, but the 1920s saw the spread of professional associations – of teachers, post office clerks, and doctors, among others – a process that effectively saw sectors of Spain's middle classes republicanize themselves in a quest for political rights. Accelerating migration to the cities in boom-time conditions and the spread of radio to educated metropolitan constituencies also dramatically increased the distance between urban Spain and the villages and small towns of *la España profunda*.

That modernity was breaking through could also be glimpsed in the dictatorship's own contradictions. In spite of Primo's brief to restore conservative order, he also sought to implement a number of key reforms in the army and the sphere of labour rights. But even a military dictatorship found itself blocked here by corporate military interests, while the landed elites thwarted the extension of key social reforms to the impoverished masses of the rural south. When army opposition finally brought Primo down in January 1930, the king found himself compromised. With a groundswell of Republican sentiment in urban Spain, the Catholic Church was the only institution of the old regime unequivocally to back the monarchy. The memory of the dangerously novel elements of the dictatorship may, paradoxically, have made the prospect of a

Republic seem less momentous to elite groups in consequence. Indeed, when the Republic was declared peacefully on 14 April 1931, it may even have been viewed as a useful means of pacifying the popular opinion represented by the jubilant crowds thronging the big city streets. But those who believed that the Republic would simply be 'business as usual' – the political order of the monarchy, without a king – were soon disabused. The first Republican administration was determined to give the new regime a content of reforming policy that would effect a fundamental redistribution of social and economic power in Spain.

Those backing a reforming agenda constituted two distinct groups. First, the progressive republicans, a political class of mainly lawyers and teachers, forming groupuscules rather than mass parties. Precisely because they lacked electoral muscle in what was now a political system based on universal suffrage, the republicans required the backing of the second group: Spain's socialist movement (political party and trade union). A historically moderate and reformist political organization, the socialists were the only mass political movement in Spain when the Republic was declared. While they were focused on social reform, wishing to introduce a mini welfare state, the republicans' objectives centred on structural reform. They saw themselves as the heirs of the 1789 revolution in France and sought to open Spain up to Europe, implementing economic and cultural modernization on the French model in four crucial respects: reform of land ownership, education, State-Church relations, and the army.

Agrarian reform was intended to create in southern Spain a smallholding peasantry with a republican allegiance whose increased purchasing power would also provide an internal market that could stimulate industrial development. Church and state were to be separated and the public subsidy to clergy phased out, thus releasing resources to fund a national system of non-religious primary education through which the republican nation would be made. Army reform was intended to bring the institution under civilian and constitutional control. Reducing the size of the top-heavy officer corps would also cut the salary bill and thus generate more funds for structural reform. All the republican reforms, as well as the social welfare legislation of their socialist colleagues, were designed to increase economic democracy as the essential prerequisite for establishing political democracy. Progressive republicans were above all constitutionalists, though they understood that many more of the economically and socially dispossessed had to be included before the Republic could effectively implement the rule of law. But understanding a situation is one thing, having the power required to implement the necessary measures is quite another.

The Republic's was an immensely ambitious programme of structural reform. Indeed, it was almost certainly too ambitious to attempt so much at one time. Even worse, the attempt was being made at a time of world economic depression, when the new government was saddled with a burden of debt from the Primo dictatorship. But it is also understandable that republicans and socialists felt there was no time to delay; it was half a century since progressive political forces had been in power – and then only very briefly, in the First Republic of 1873. So the perceived backlog of reform (again viewed in comparative European perspective) was considerable. However, the inherent complexity of structural reform combined with the difficulties the government had in finding experienced personnel – also unsurprising given the Left's long exclusion from power – only added to the problems rapidly gathering on the new political horizon.

For, inevitably, the reforms raised opposition among Spain's traditional elites. The response of the ecclesiastical hierarchy struck an apocalyptic note even before the Republic had begun to make policy. The pastoral letter issued by the Cardinal Primate on 1 May 1931 contained an incendiary royalist homily that caused the government to require him to leave Spain. His call to the faithful to mobilize in spiritual and patriotic rearmament came close to declaring the Republic an illegitimate regime. Moreover, the public words of other bishops did so overtly when they described the Republic as the triumph of error and sin.

A strain of ideological apocalypse was evident too among sectors of Spain's military elites. Since the end of empire the officer corps had become an increasingly self-enclosed caste. The military academies overwhelmingly favoured the sons of officers. The daughters of officers married into military families. This was a world where people had fewer and fewer personal ties to other social groups. A new, small-scale colonial venture was begun in Morocco in the early years of the 20th century. But the experience of the North African campaigns forged a brand of warrior nationalism that only further hardened military attitudes. Indeed, it was among the officers who made their careers in the colonial Army of Africa, including Francisco Franco himself, that there would emerge the most fatally reductive views of what was wrong with metropolitan Spanish society and politics.

When in 1927 Franco took charge of Spain's main military academy at Zaragoza, he put in place a teaching staff dominated by these colonial officers, the *Africanistas*. The academy became the forcing ground for ideas of imperial rebirth, of the military as the guardian and saviour of Spain, and was thus an integral part of an emergent politics of the ultra-nationalist right. The idea of a squad of soldiers 'saving civilization' would be given its final and most extreme form by European fascism in the 1930s. José Antonio Primo de Rivera, the leader of Spain's fascist party, the Falange, quoted Oswald Spengler's classic formulation from *The Decline of the West* (vol. 2, 1922) – a text that, like the *Africanistas*' own remedies, was a pathological symptom of social change rather than the solution it proclaimed. One of the Republican government's very first decisions in June 1931 was to close down the Zaragoza military academy. It also froze battlefield promotions made during the Moroccan campaigns, thus enraging the *Africanistas*. Not only were many officers hostile to the Republic's goal of imposing civilian and constitutional control on the army, they also found it affronting their ultra-centralist principles. For the republicans and socialists, though quite centralist-minded themselves, were prepared to devolve some political powers to the historic nationalities of the Basque Country and Catalonia as an exercise in regime-building and democratic good faith.

But questions of political culture and ideology aside, a no less crucial issue for young army officers was that of salaries and career prospects. Republican reforms would inevitably curtail both. Even the military dictatorship of the 1920s had come adrift when it attempted to interfere with army prerogatives. This did not bode well for despised civilian politicians – republicans to boot – who were bidding to reform the army head on. In the end, the coup of July 1936 would find its most consistent supporters in this junior officer class which stood to lose most materially and was also profoundly hostile to the idea of a pluralist democracy. But these officers stood to lose no more in 1936 than they had in 1932 when a first coup attempt was tried, unsuccessfully. Nor was the apocalyptic strain necessarily headier later rather than earlier. Something had certainly changed, though mainly this did not have to do with the military. What would eventually 'arm' the military coup of July 1936 was the emergence and growth of mass political opposition to Republican reforms among civilian sectors in Spanish society.

Resistance to reform came, then, not only from Spain's old elites. People of the middling sort in the centre-north conservative heartland also began to raise their voices against the new Republic. This mainly had to do with the Church. The Republic's secularizing reforms upset deeply Catholic sensibilities in this region. There was always going to be ecclesiastical opposition to measures such as the separation of Church and State. But what caused most popular offence was the Republic's interference with the Catholic culture that framed social identities and daily life: for example, the way the new authorities restricted religious processions or the ringing of church bells, or their interference with ceremonies and celebrations organized around local saints or local appellations of the Virgin Mary. This was a world of private and family devotions, but also of communal piety, where deeply felt emotions had as much to do with an allegiance to a way of life and a specific place (the immediate locality or *patria chica*) as with religious faith or spirituality *per se*. Or rather, loyalty to these things was indivisible.

It was because these local worlds were felt to be threatened – by Republican reform, but also by larger processes of accelerating social and economic change of which the Republic was seen to be a part – that religious revival played such a significant part in popular opposition to the new regime. At Ezkioga in the Basque Country there were new Marian apparitions in 1931, when people reported seeing visions of the Virgin Mary. Large pilgrimages ensued. As the social history of 19th- and 20th-century Europe shows, religious visions tend to occur at times of trauma-inducing upheaval. Common triggers are economic crises, epidemics, war, and political persecution. Although it is not usually a conscious process, religion then takes on an additionally powerful meaning, as a defence against new and frightening things. The Republic's phasing out of the secular clergy's stipend also alienated many poorer priests who had not necessarily been irreconcilable opponents. But Catholic mobilization in 1930s Spain was predominantly that of lay people who, well before the Civil War itself, came to see themselves as engaged on a crusade to defend an endangered way of life. This was equally true whether in the rural fastnesses of northern Navarre where the quasi-theocratic Carlists, radically opposed to all manifestations of social and cultural modernity, were training their militia, or among Catholic youth in provincial towns and even the big cities who became activists in the new mass organizations of the Right. This mobilization included – paradoxically – support for votes for women, while progressive republicans were far more hostile to female enfranchisement, believing that the greater influence of Catholicism among female constituencies would bring a bloc vote for conservative candidates. (Women would vote for the first time in Spain in November 1933.) Certainly the religious issue could be manipulated, as it was when the large landowners of the south successfully used it to mobilize poor northern smallholders against an agrarian reform that damaged only their own interests. The politics of mass popular conservatism were, nevertheless, more than the product of elite manipulation. It is equally true, however, that the political forms of this new conservative mobilization would have been inconceivable without the well-established organizational networks of the Catholic Church in Spain.

Republican reformers got the worst of all worlds. They legislated to debar the religious orders from teaching, believing that they represented an insuperable barrier to the creation of a republican nation in Spain. But in practice, as a result of both subterfuge and legal delays, the attempted debarment failed. When the Civil War erupted in the summer of 1936 there still had not been a period of Republican government when religious personnel had actually ceased to teach in Spain. Yet, in attempting such an exclusion, the republicans had mobilized a powerful coalition of conservative forces against themselves. Given budgetary constraints too, it is hard to see how the Republic could in the short term have entirely replaced the Church's role in primary education.

Republican secularization was, then, impolitic, ill thought-out, and largely counter-productive. Some commentators have also argued that it was ethically questionable – all the more so given that the Republic had staked its own legitimacy on constitutional principles. But this is less straightforward than they imply. Polemics about secularization are very much still alive in politically liberal and culturally diverse Western societies of the 21st century, yet few would suggest that their basic constitutional credentials are negated thereby. Not 'liberalism' nor 'constitutionalism' nor 'democracy' are free-floating concepts; all have to be understood and interrogated in specific historical contexts. Conservative Catholics in 1930s Spain were outraged that their beliefs and practices were being constrained, but they themselves entertained no concept of civil and cultural rights within the Spanish state for those professing other religions, still less for freethinkers or atheists.

The ultimate political irony is that the Spanish Right of the 1930s, which was fundamentally hostile to the notion of progressive democratic change, learned to operate very successfully in the new political environment of the Republic in order to put a brake on that change. The political Left, on the other hand, proved far less successful or adaptable. Why should this have been so?

From the start, the Left was handicapped by the great ideological differences between its constituent parts. Widest of all was the gap between the parliamentary socialist movement and the anti-parliamentary anarcho-syndicalist CNT. These differences were not a matter of voluntarism or sheer bloody-mindedness, as the standard historical narrative so often implies. Rather, their irreducibility was a result of the vastly different political, economic, and cultural experiences of the Left's social constituencies in what was a highly unevenly developed country. For example, the direct political action favoured by many anarcho-syndicalists instantly recommended itself to the unskilled and the landless poor, whose lack of bargaining power and social defencelessness made socialist promises of gradual change through the ballot box seem immensely improbable, if not downright incredible.

Also confronting republicans and socialists was the enormous gap between political authority and real power. The new government had the legitimacy invested in it by the democratic electoral process. It could pass legislation in the Madrid parliament. But ensuring its implementation beyond that parliament was quite another matter. Part of the problem was a lack of trained personnel, but a far greater difficulty was the entrenched opposition of elites who had lost none of their social or economic power. This was true above all in the rural south, where large landowners called upon the local civil guard to discipline recalcitrant workers after 14 April 1931 just as they had done before. Police personnel remained unchanged and were thus still enmeshed in clientelistic relations with the local elites. Landowners also refused to recognize crucial pieces of redistributive social welfare legislation, effectively 'locking out' workers by leaving land uncultivated. Estate henchmen also meted out violence – sometimes with fatal results – to trade union officials who came to monitor the new measures. The political temperature in the southern countryside went up because the very fact of the Republic's birth had raised expectations among the poor and the dispossessed. (If for many Catholics the Republic was Antichrist, for these people it was conceived of as a source of Messianic salvation.) But the tension also rose because of the sheer vindictiveness of the opponents of reform, who flung at the frequently (still) unemployed and hungry taunts such as 'let the Republic feed you' (*comed República*).

The thwarting of popular aspirations for social change produced disillusion not only among the landless poor and unemployed of the rural south exasperated by the durability of the old relations of power, but also among worker constituencies in urban Spain. Here the effects of the depression were beginning to bite. Unemployment was rising, especially among the unskilled, such as building labourers, who had flocked to the cities in the boom years of the 1920s. Many were now living below the level of subsistence. But the Republic's ability to mitigate the situation through social welfare was limited. It was mainly the republicans rather than the socialists who controlled financial policy – and they were monetarists rather than Keynesians. The only policy area in which they were prepared to spend was in education, where they borrowed substantially to fund their school-building programme. The republican-socialist government did more in relative terms to deliver social welfare than any previous administration. Ironically, it was in part the huge level of popular expectation of the Republic that saw this achievement interpreted as a policy failure.

But political alienation also occurred because the weight of Republican law and order fell on constituencies of the poor and marginal. While the Right complained incessantly in parliament about the Republic's public order deficit, the unemployed and the working poor could tell a very different story. On numerous notorious occasions, in urban and rural settings across Spain, Republican security forces clashed fatally with protesting workers: at Castilblanco in December 1931; in Arnedo (Logroño) and Llobregat (Barcelona province) both in January 1932; and at Casas Viejas (Andalusia) in January 1933. Beneath these high-profile incidents there lay a daily experience of repression and exclusion. The new urban police force created by the Republic evicted rent strikers and, in response to complaints from shopkeepers and the Chamber of Commerce, cleared the streets of itinerant street traders selling cheap food to the poor and marginal. Such incidents reinforced the claims of the Republic's radical Left critics – especially the anarchists – that nothing had changed, that parliament and legislative reform was a sham that could never benefit the have-nots. With reform being blocked in the localities, and with the depression taking its toll in rural and urban Spain, the strains on constitutional democracy began to tell. It was hard for the republicans credibly to demand respect for the rules of the game from those who on a daily basis were being excluded from it by the denial of their social and economic rights as citizens. These were, moreover, rights that were supposed to be guaranteed by the constitution and the law.

The situation worsened after divisions on the Left saw a conservative government returned to power in November 1933. Reforms on the statute book were a dead letter. The elites sought to roll back even the small amount of redistributive change that had been pushed through in the localities. It is in the context of explosive anger and frustration at the backlash against reform that we have to understand the mounting strikes and protests of 1934. Both the Left's youth movements and radicalized Catholic conservative and fascist youth took politics into the city streets. Not only was the space of Spanish politics shifting, but the mobilization of the young across the political spectrum – and of young women in particular – was tranforming its very nature.

The frustrations on the Left culminated in October 1934 in an attempt to launch a revolutionary general strike. This ran out of steam even in Madrid, where radicalized sectors of the socialist youth movement took the lead. But the northern coal-mining region of Asturias, with its contentious history of labour relations and hard hit by recession, exploded into armed rebellion. The miners held out for two weeks, but their villages were bombed by the Spanish airforce, the coastal towns shelled by the navy, and the valleys finally overrun by the Spanish army. A harsh and extensive repression ensued throughout Asturias in which General Franco, as *de facto* head of the war ministry, deployed both native Moroccan troops and the Foreign Legion, fearing that Spanish conscripts were not to be trusted politically. Constitutional guarantees were suspended across Spain. The impact on the Left was catastrophic. Thirty thousand people were imprisoned and many of them tortured. Party and union premises were closed and the Left's press silenced. Socialist town councils were overthrown, civil servants of liberal or left opinions were discriminated against, and everywhere employers and management took the opportunity to dismiss trade unionists and left activists *en masse*.

The events of October 1934 are often cited by historians as evidence that the Spanish Left could not be trusted to play by the democratic rules. But this assessment takes no account of the complexity of the events leading to October – not least the conservative government's own flouting of the law as it sought to brake or reverse social reform. It also ignores the obvious lesson to be drawn from what happened in Asturias: that, in fact, the Left had no other option but to work for social change through legal, parliamentary channels. For in any showdown of physical force it simply could not prevail. Even the history of more minor confrontations between workers and the state since 1931 indicated this. After October 1934 this was clear not only to Spain's socialist leaders (even those who continued to employ a radical rhetoric for strategic purposes) but also to large numbers of ordinary people who supported them. This realization, and an awareness of the need for political unity on the Left, gave birth to a new electoral coalition of progressive forces that won the elections in February 1936 on a ticket of re-enacting the parliamentary reform programme of 1931–3.

It was at this point that the military stepped in. Not to prevent 'revolution', as they claimed, but to block the road to constitutional and legislative reform that the parliamentary Right had now evidently failed to stop by legal means – since they had lost the February elections. The spring and summer of 1936 saw the rapprochement of the military and civilian Right and also of patrician and radical conservatives, as the leader of Spain's fascist party pledged allegiance to a military coup.

What might progressive forces on the Left have done to defuse the situation? A government reinforced by the parliamentary socialist party would have been an improvement on the timorous all-republican cabinet, whose members seemed incapable of decisive action even though by the spring of 1936 it was an open secret that a military coup was being planned. But the socialists had their own problems: there were deep internal political splits in the movement. And just like the republicans, the socialist leaders – for all their progressive social policies – were, ironically, less than comfortable with the new politics of mass mobilization that the Republic had ushered in.

The challenges that beset Spain's new democracy in the 1930s were complex and deep-rooted and thus not susceptible to rapid resolution. In so far as the Republic can be said to have 'failed' (another historiographical commonplace), then its failure was a quite specific one: it proved unable to prevent sectors of the officer corps from making a coup. It is not the business of historians to engage in counterfactual speculation, but one could argue that what established the preconditions for a successful coup attempt was not Spain's deep tensions, but republican-socialist failure to implement key policy reforms in 1931–3: most crucially, perhaps, the failure to demilitarize public order. But, as historians also know, the benefit of hindsight is really only the dangerous illusion of twenty-twenty vision.

All those who supported Spain's military rebels had in common a fear of where change was leading – whether their fears were of material or psychological loss (wealth, professional status, established social and political hierarchies, religious or sexual/gendered certainties). The 1930s in Spain saw the development of a series of culture wars that would play out during the years of the Civil War itself. As in all culture wars, the way people mythologized their fears generated violence.

But what allowed any of this to occur at all was the military coup. Its original act of violence was that it killed off the possibility of other forms of peaceful political evolution. The military rebellion imposed the battle lines, but their meaning was not fixed on 18 July 1936. The meaning of the war would be made by its political protagonists and victims; its volunteer and conscript soldiers, by war workers and draft dodgers, by refugees; by all those who participated in or endured the ensuing three years of conflict.

The mechanism of a coup gave the July rising against mass democracy a traditional political veneer. But the quasi-social Darwinist mission of the military rebels hatched in colonial North Africa, to conquer and purify metropolitan Spain – which will be discussed in the next chapter – indicated something violently new.

So too did the rapprochement between the 'squad of soldiers' and Spanish fascism. In the ultimate paradox, the modernity of the July coup was also inscribed in the rebels' public declaration at the time of the rising. They justified their action by reference to its support by Spanish society as a whole. Their own language thus inadvertently acknowledged the depth of the post-Enlightenment social and political change that they were seeking to reverse in Spain.

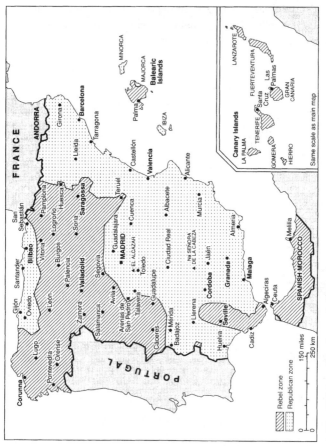

1. The division of Spain, 22 July 1936

Chapter 2
Rebellion, revolution, and repression

Every age remains in the memory of future generations. But every age has its own internal logic, its own structure of feeling.

(J. Ugarte Tellería, *La nueva Covadonga insurgente*)

The military coup against the Republic began on 17 July 1936 among elements of the colonial army based in Spanish North Africa (Morocco). A day later the rebellion spread to mainland Spain in the form of provincial garrison revolts. It was both a failure and a success; it failed to take over the whole of the country at a stroke, as had been the rebels' intention, but it did succeed in paralysing the Republican regime, and, crucially, deprived it of the means of organizing rapid, effective resistance. The rebellion shattered the command structure of the army, leaving the Madrid government without troops and unsure of which officers it could trust. The simultaneous collapse of the police compounded these already grave problems, creating a vacuum of authority in most Republican-held areas that had no parallel in the rebel zone, where the military took control from the outset. In spite of regime collapse, however, loyal elements in the police joined forces with the worker militia, formed by trade unions and political parties of the Left to meet the emergency; together they were able to quell the garrison revolts in most of urban industrial Spain.

2. Rebel soldiers enter a town in southern Spain in the opening stages of the Civil War. The children who have joined the procession carry an image of the Sacred Heart of Jesus – an old religious symbol now mediating a new form of mass conservative mobilization.

The initial division of Spanish territory between Republic and rebels (see Figure 1) reflected the political geography of the country. The rebellion generally tended to fail in areas where there was significant support for Republican reforms and/or a progressive political agenda more broadly. So urban centres with their high concentration of workers in organized labour movements were mainly held by the Republic – although some exceptions obtained, most notably Seville in the southwest, where General Queipo de Llano unleashed the bulk of his garrison, some 5,800 troops, against the city's labour movement. Elsewhere in the countryside of the deep south, the presence of thousands of landless peasants was initially a factor inhibiting the success of the coup, while on the northeast seaboard, Catalonia and the Valencian region, with their confederal past and strong anti-centralist sentiment, would remain Republican throughout the war.

The areas that came immediately under the control of the military

The Spanish Civil War

22

rebels tended to be those that had returned conservative majorities in the February 1936 elections. This meant mainly the rural, smallholding centre-north and northwest of Spain. In these areas a significant measure of popular support for the military coup derived from the hostility to the Republic's secularization programme felt by the peasantry and the conservative provincial middling classes. (The case of the Basque Country in northern Spain was exceptional, because there strong support for a regional nationalist agenda of political autonomy aligned even social conservatives against the ultra-centralist military rebels.)

But the logic of pre-war political geography is not the whole explanation for the territorial disposition emerging after 18 July. No area of Spain was entirely and homogenously conservative. Even in their heartland the military rebels still had violently to repress some civilian sectors that resisted; as happened with port workers in the northwest town of Vigo in Galicia. Bloody repression also acted as a force of coercion more broadly. For example, people in villages and small towns who had entertained vague Republican sympathies suddenly felt compelled to align themselves publicly with the new rebel authorities in order to protect their families, even if this sometimes meant betraying friendships and personal allegiances. The film *Butterfly's Tongue* (*La Lengua de las Mariposas*) (1999), based on a short story by the Galician writer Manuel Rivas, recounts a deadly example of this phenomenon. A young boy is required by his mother to participate in the public humiliation and detention of his beloved Republican schoolmaster in order to distract attention from his own father's freethinking past. So we see the complex and contradictory motives that so often lay behind the apparently binary choices made by people in the wake of the rebellion. Indeed, this enforced reductiveness, the obligation to 'take sides', constitutes the coup's first, and most enduring, act of violence.

In order to make their coup viable, the military rebels also had to remove, and frequently to kill, a significant number of senior army officers who refused to support them. In part because of this the rebels too faced a certain degree of military dislocation – a shattered army cut both ways. Nor could the lack of an integrated fighting force be compensated for by the right-wing political militias of Carlists and Falangists rapidly mobilizing in rebel territory.

The division of Spain resulting from the botched coup initially appeared to favour the Republic. It held the capital city of Madrid, which lay at the heart of the country's communications network and also contained its gold reserves. With most of the big urban centres, the Republic also had control of industry. For the rebels time was of the essence; unless they could rapidly galvanize and augment their forces, the Republic would likely be able to regroup its own and thus stifle the rebellious garrisons.

It was at this point – some seven days on from the initial coup – that international intervention first became a factor in the conflict. Facing likely defeat, the military rebels requested and received planes from Hitler and Mussolini to transport their crack troops, the Foreign Legion and the Army of Africa, across the Straits of Gibraltar to mainland Spain. (The Straits were temporarily blockaded by the Republican navy, which had mutinied against its pro-rebel commanders.) In this first act of international intervention, which also constituted the first airlift of troops in the history of modern warfare, Europe's fascist powers gave the Spanish rebels their army, allowing them to launch a full-scale war against the Republic. Hitler and Mussolini agreed to intervene at the same time, but each made his decision independently. Neither dictator was intending to become embroiled in a long war, rather they were offering planes to achieve what they calculated could be a rapid rebel victory. This would guarantee a friendly Spain and thus serve their strategic interests.

But things did not go according to plan – not least because of Republican resistance. This was a phenomenon significantly driven by the popular desire to protect social and economic advances associated with the Republic. Frequently too there was a desire to accelerate these into a revolutionary new order. This was possible at least for a time in the approximate two-thirds of Spain remaining to the Republic precisely because the coup had induced the collapse of the regime. The government's writ did not run beyond the capital city of Madrid. The normal functions of government were in abeyance; the paralysis of police and army also gave a huge impetus to localism. It could scarcely have been otherwise in a country still so marked by the invertebrateness deriving from uneven economic development, where allegiance remained to the immediate community (*patria chica*) as the lived unit of experience. In some places every village made its own revolution, organizing its life independently of everywhere else. The American writer Gamel Woolsey was living in a village near the southern city of Málaga when the war broke out. She noted in her diary how well this isolation suited its inhabitants, who distrusted all 'foreigners' – that is to say, all Spaniards not born in the village, and for whom Málaga itself seemed as socially and culturally distant as Madrid or Barcelona.

To many in the worker militia too – whether in Málaga, Madrid, or Barcelona – this centrifugal explosion was a positive development. For urban and rural workers, and for the poor more generally in Spain, the state still had overwhelmingly negative connotations: military conscription, indirect taxation, and everyday persecution – particularly for the unionized. Thus for many Spanish workers, resistance to the military rebels was initially also directed 'against the state' and was bound up with building a new social and political order, often on radical anti-capitalist economic lines (money was frequently abolished). In urban and rural northeast Spain (Barcelona and Aragon) and in Republican parts of the rural south, industry and agriculture were collectivized, and trade union and party committees organized emergency defence and met the needs of their neighbourhood or village.

Nor, outside of the bigger towns and cities, was political sectarianism between organizations of the Left yet that much in evidence. Otherwise it would have been inconceivable that a member of the CNT from a village in Valencia province could in 1936 have named his baby daughter after Stalin. This absence of sectarianism indicates that at the start of the war political organizations of the Left often had only a tenuous organizational presence outside the main urban centres. But even as this changed across the war, the appearance of sectarian divisions was still more frequently about the grafting of new labels onto older local political disputes, or else the result of specific tensions produced by the material difficulties of the war, than it was strictly ideological in origin. The new collective and cooperative structures appearing in the summer of 1936 were, nevertheless, an attempt to resolve the key social and political conflicts of the pre-war Republican period (1931–6). In the process, the balance of social, economic, and political power was shifted in many communities.

This shift was produced in a rather darker way too by a wave of violence. The absence of a functioning police force or judiciary in Republican territory in the first weeks after the coup, plus the *de facto* amnesties that saw gaols empty, made it possible for all manner of personal scores to be settled and acts of outright criminality to be pursued in the guise of revolutionary justice. As the war escalated across its first eight months, some acts of violence in Republican Spain would also be triggered by the terrifying experience of aerial bombardment as well as by rumours of mass shootings and other atrocities in rebel territory.

But the acts of violence committed by ordinary people in Republican territory immediately after the military rising had a clearly discernible political dimension. Their actions were triggered by anger at what was seen as the rebels' attempt to put the clock back by force to old regime order. Avenging violence was directed at the sources and bearers of the old power – whether material (by destroying property records and land registries) or human (the assassination or brutalization of priests, civil guards, police, employers, and estate bailiffs). So there was a clear link between post-coup violence and pre-war conflicts: for example, over the blocking of land or labour reform legislation or worker dismissals after the general strikes of 1934, or over conflicts (again, concerning the non-implementation of social and labour reforms) in the aftermath of the February 1936 elections.

The forms this violence took were often highly theatrical – ritualized even – which indicates other things too. First and foremost it had a symbolic charge: people were not only killing or humiliating their human enemy but also attacking feared or oppressive sources of power and authority in which they saw the individual victim embedded. This is part of the explanation for why 'benevolent' employers or 'good' priests became targets. Indeed, the best-known, if far from the only, example of symbolic killing in Republican Spain was anticlerical violence on an unprecedented scale which claimed the lives of nearly seven thousand (overwhelmingly male) religious personnel. Priests and monks were killed because they were seen as representing an oppressive Church historically associated with the rich and powerful whose ecclesiastical hierarchy had backed the military rebellion. The laity too were sometimes engulfed by this anticlerical anger. As one oral testimony has recalled, the church singer and the bell-ringer were part of an old world that had to be annihilated. Nor was the paradox of an inherently religious component to anticlerical violence less true in Spain than elsewhere. The act of desecration itself – churches destroyed or turned to profane uses; the remains of religious personnel disinterred – speaks eloquently of the power still invested in religion and the Church by the desecrators themselves.

In retrospect, little remains inexplicable about ordinary people's impulse to violence in Republican territory. But the fact of its occurrence seriously damaged the Republic's credibility abroad at precisely the moment when it needed to call on external support to confront the mounting military challenge posed by the rebels. For republican and socialist leaders who had staked the Republic's legitimacy on its defence of constitutional forms and the rule of law, the knowledge that they had been powerless to prevent extra-judicial killing was devastating. (Although there were many instances of individual political leaders intervening to save lives.) It was their determination to end uncontrolled violence that provided a powerful ethical drive to the bid to restore the authority of the central Republican government in the face of coup-induced fragmentation.

For their part, the rebels publicly justified their coup as a bid to forestall a violent revolution by the Left. But, again in retrospect, we can see that it was the military rebellion itself that created the conditions for violence on such a scale and not only in Republican territory. In the days and weeks after the July coup, public declarations were made by local civilian elites in the rebel zone – whether bosses of the fascist Falange or people associated with the mass Catholic party, CEDA, or monarchist landowners or businessmen or clerics. These were made independently of each other and of the military authorities, but they were remarkably similar. Their message was that Spain needed to be purged or purified. Sometimes they even spoke of the need for a blood sacrifice. These kinds of sentiments unleashed a savage repression that happened from the outset everywhere in rebel Spain, including in many areas where the military rebels were in control from the start, where there was no armed resistance, no political resistance to speak of either, no 'front', no advancing or retreating troops–in short, where there was no 'war' according to a conventional definition of the term. What there was, however, was a culture war that the perpetrators carried in their heads. The coup had sanctioned its unleashing and thus opened the way to mass murder.

The impulse to kill was driven even more clearly than it was in Republican territory by a manichaean mindset historically associated with certain forms of Catholic culture and practice. The perpetrators in the rebel zone would have perceived their own motivations to be completely different from those of the Republican 'enemy'. But the driving force of violence was similarly the annihilation of the other. While in Republican territory the objective for some individuals was millenarian – killing as a means of achieving *tabula rasa* and with it a brave new world – in rebel areas killing was widely perceived as a cleansing action designed to rid the community of sources of 'pollution' and the dangers they supposed.

People of all ages and conditions fell victim to this 'cleansing'. What they had in common was that they were perceived as representing the changes brought by the Republic. This did not just mean the politically active – although Republican members of parliament or village mayors were primary targets for liquidation if caught. Nor did it only mean those who had benefited materially from the Republic's redistributive reforms – though urban workers, tenant farmers, and agricultural labourers were killed in their thousands. It also meant 'cleansing' people who symbolized cultural change and thus posed a threat to old ways of being and thinking: progressive teachers, intellectuals, self-educated workers, 'new' women. Rebel violence was targeted against the socially, culturally, and sexually different.

It saw the deaths in Zamora of Amparo Barayón, wife of the Republican novelist Ramón Sender, a woman whose independent spirit was considered a 'sin' against traditional gender norms; in Granada of the poet Federico García Lorca – killed both for his political beliefs and for his sexuality; and of many thousands of less well-known Spaniards, like Pilar Espinosa from Candeleda in Avila, taken away by a Falangist death squad because she read the socialist party newspaper and was known to 'have ideas' (*tener ideas*), thinking for oneself being considered doubly reprehensible in women.

3. **Amparo Barayón, photographed here in the 'flapper' fashion of the 1920s, was a victim of extra-judicial execution in the rebel zone. Franco's forces saw their war as a crusade against social and cultural change.**

Those who did the killing in rebel Spain during the first months were mainly vigilantes. What occurred was a massacre of civilians by other civilians. Mostly this took the form of death squads abducting people from their homes or else taking them out of prison. In a majority of cases the assassins had close links to rightist political organizations that had backed the coup, in particular the fascist Falange. But the military authorities made no attempt to reign in this terror. In fact the killers were often acting with the connivance of the authorities, otherwise the death squads who came for Amparo Barayón and thousands of her compatriots would never have been able to take their victims out of gaol at will.

This points to the fundamental asymmetry between the violence occurring in Republican and rebel zones. The military authorities had the resources to stem the violence – for there was no collapse of the police or public order in rebel areas. But they chose not to. Why they did not reveals a great deal about the political dynamic taking shape in rebel Spain. The military were of course unconcerned about the unconstitutionalism of extra-judicial murder *per se*. For those who had rebelled against the Republic, liberal politics, constitutionalism, and the language of rights were perceived as the problem not the solution. Moreover, those being removed by the death squads were part of the same 'problem', for the military too spoke the language of purification. Local ties, the bonds of friendship – occasionally even family – also linked the military to the vigilantes. But, above all, terror was seen as the first stage in the crucial reimposition of 'order'. First, it was intended to teach those who had believed in the Republic as a vehicle of change that their aspirations would always be bought at too high a price. So the violence was a way of shaking up society while staving off the redistribution of social and economic power heralded by the Republic. Second – although this was not necessarily a conscious intention – a crucial complicity was created between the rebel authorities and those sectors of the population that engaged in or connived at the repression of their friends, neighbours, and family members. This complicity began to lay the foundations, bottom up, of a new rebel state and social order.

Also vital to the military's extension of control was the way the repression annihilated 'home' as a safe space. When the coup occurred there was a strong belief among those who felt threatened that if they could get back to their place of origin, their village, their *patria chica*, there they would be safe from the vicious fall-out of national political divisions. So many of the victims of extra-judicial killing in rebel territory – whether famous or anonymous – died precisely because they went home. Only there they discovered that 'home' no longer existed: the originary violence of the military coup meant precisely that nothing could exist outside the brutal political binary it had imposed.

The nature of the rebels' project became absolutely clear once the Army of Africa landed in the south of mainland Spain at the end of July 1936. The Army of Africa was composed of the professional soldiers of the Foreign Legion plus a fighting force of Moroccan mercenaries commanded by Spanish career officers (*Africanistas*), and was headed by General Francisco Franco. Workers and other civilian defenders had no adequate means of resisting it. During August and September 1936, Franco's forces swept up through southern Spain *en route* for the central capital city of Madrid. In its wake the repression escalated as the Army strategically butchered and terrorized the pro-Republican population, especially the rural landless. For this initial phase of the Civil War in the south was also part of the 'solution' to pre-war conflicts. It was a war of agrarian counter-reform that turned Andalusia and Extremadura into killing fields. The large landowners who owned the vast estates which covered most of the southern half of Spain rode along with the Army of Africa to reclaim by force of arms the land on which the Republic had settled the landless poor. Rural labourers were killed where they stood, the 'joke' being they had got their 'land reform' at last – in the form of a burial plot.

In villages across the rebel-held south there was systematic brutality, torture, shaving and rape of women, and mass public killings of both men and women in the aftermath of conquest. Sometimes villages were literally wiped off the map by repression. The war was being fought as if it were a colonial campaign against insubordinate indigenous peoples. Spain's landed aristocracy, often the fathers and elder brothers of *Africanista* army officers, viewed the landless poor of the south as virtual slaves without humanity or rights. Franco, although from more modest provincial origins in northern Spain, had himself spent ten and a half years in Spanish

North Africa, making his military career there in the brutal colonial war. Long before the Italians in Ethiopia (if not before the British in Mesopotamia), Spain had used poisonous gas, of German manufacture, against its colonial population in Morocco. Franco's frequent requests to Italy for chemical weapons in the course of 1936 and 1937, even if strategic considerations eventually precluded their use, reflected his earlier experiences in North Africa.

Later, Franco would declare that his experience in Africa had made possible his 'salvation' of Spain in 1936: 'without Africa I cannot explain myself to myself or to my comrades in arms'. In a letter he wrote on 11 August 1936 to General Mola, the commander of the rebels' northern forces, he stressed the need to annihilate all resistance in the 'occupied zones'. This comment encapsulates the political beliefs not only of Franco but of a whole cohort of conservative officers. Spain had been 'occupied' by alien political ideas and forms of social organization that threatened the 'Spain' of unity, hierarchy, and cultural homogeneity in which they believed and which they saw it as their duty to defend. On 27 July, Franco was interviewed by the North American journalist Jay Allen, whose report three weeks later on the massacre of Republican defenders in the southern town of Badajoz would catapult the Spanish war into newspaper headlines throughout Europe and America. In the July interview Franco brushed aside the reporter's questions about the high level of resistance the rebels had encountered, declaring 'I will save Spain from Marxism whatever the cost'. To Allen's quizzical 'And if that means shooting half of Spain?', Franco replied 'As I said, whatever the cost'. The rebels' contempt for constitutional politics, their preparedness to use mass executions and terror throughout the war meant that they, unlike the Republicans, never faced the dilemma of how to deal with the 'enemy within'. In spite of this the military rebels received very little bad press in the mainstream media beyond Spain. Among the reasons for this was one immensely powerful one: the legitimation of the coup provided by the Catholic Church.

The rebels' uncompromising belief in the need to rid society of political and cultural 'pollutants' reinforced at the outset the public backing given to the rebels by the hierarchy of the Spanish Church. This led rapidly to the presentation of their war effort as a crusade. First codified in a pastoral letter at the end of September 1936, the Church's imprimature sanctioned the coup in the eyes of conservative establishments across Europe and beyond, and was thus an immensely valuable propaganda device. Nevertheless, it was not without its problems for the rebels, not the least of which was the enormous and evident contradiction of a latter-day Catholic crusade whose front-line troops were Islamic mercenaries. Military and ecclesiastical spokesmen both waxed lyrical about the cleansing services offered by the African soldiers – their underlying racism buried beneath the image of these troops as part of a larger imperial enterprise that was 'essentially' Christian. This led to some remarkable verbal contortions in the reports of the Spanish journalists accompanying the colonial Army during its southern march:

> at the hour of liberation [of the Toledo garrison siege in September 1936] women of Castile received from African hands a bread as white as Communion bread . . . [the war] was a Mudejar enterprise against the Asiatic hordes.

The question of race and racism here would, however, remain below the political surface for the duration of the war. The Spanish Left had never developed an anticolonialist discourse. Its opposition to the war in North Africa had always been based on a defence of Spanish workers' rights (as the soldiers who died in these campaigns) rather than on the wrongs of colonization. Indeed, Republican attitudes to Franco's North African soldiers, whom they understandably feared, were scarcely less racist than those of the rebels themselves. Nor during the Civil War was the Republic ever able successfully to elaborate a strategic anticolonialism. Some expression of political sympathy for embryonic Moroccan nationalism might potentially have helped to choke Franco's supply of troops. But no such initiative was seriously contemplated for fear of upsetting Britain and France, as senior colonial powers on whose support the Spanish Republicans were pinning their hopes – especially once the scale of German and Italian fascist aid to the rebels had become evident.

This aid – particularly in the form of planes and tanks – guaranteed the Army of Africa a lightning progress up through the south. It was this scenario – fascist technical support, a professional fighting force, and the attendant military victories – that explains Franco's own increasing prominence. The nominal leader of the rebellion, General Emilio Mola, whose campaign had stalled in the mountains north of Madrid, lacked the cachet of victory. The deaths of a number of other front-rank military conspirators also removed potential rivals. But Franco was at this stage still very much first among equals rather than the outstanding leader. His subsequent ascendancy was, as we shall see, the result of careful planning by his advisors, who built on the General's own eye for a strategic political opportunity. What allowed Franco to avail himself of such opportunities was, however, his spectacular progress in the south.

The Army of Africa seemed unstoppable. This should not surprise us, however, since what it faced was not a 'militia' force, as is often claimed, but rather the civilian population armed with whatever they could lay their hands on. They were pitted in open country against troops, artillery, and German and Italian air bombardments. Every time the rebel army took a centre of population, atrocities ensued. Victims' bodies were left for days in the streets to terrorize the population and then heaped together in the cemetery and burned without burial rites. As reports of these events mounted, even the rumoured threat of being outflanked was enough to send the Republicans fleeing, abandoning their weapons as they ran. On 3 September 1936 the rebels took Talavera de la Reina, the last important town separating them from the capital, Madrid. In a bare month they had advanced almost 500 kilometres. A vast tide of refugees fled northwards before Franco's army.

Thousands of Spanish workers had committed their energies and in many cases given their lives to achieving the social transformation of collectivization in the Republican south and elsewhere. But these radical initiatives remained locally focused and highly fragmented. While the enemy had also been 'local' – that is, the soldiery of the provincial garrison or (sometimes) the local police – this had not mattered. But once German and Italian intervention transformed the nature of the conflict by transporting a professional army to Spain, then the Republicans were forced to rethink their resistance strategy. It was a lesson paid for in blood by the thousands of men and women who fought and died in the south. If the Republic was to survive the rebel onslaught of modern, mechanized warfare, courtesy of German and Italian aid, it would need to put an army in the field and to mobilize its whole population for war – something unprecedented in Spanish experience. The revolutionary energy of the politically conscious, organized working class no longer sufficed as it had done in the period of street fighting against rebellious garrisons. Now everyone had to be brought on board – the politically unmobilized sectors of the population, middle-class sectors, and especially their female constituencies, in order to mount a modern war effort. Otherwise the Republic would not survive.

Chapter 3
Mobilize and survive: the Republic at war

Our modest task . . . is to organise the Apocalypse
(André Malraux, *L'Espoir*)

The rapid mobilization of the Republic's domestic resources –
human and material – was made doubly crucial in view of its
international isolation. When the coup occurred the Republican
government had straightaway attempted (19 July) to secure military
aid from the Western democracies – Britain and France. But it came
up against British hostility and French reluctance (after an initial
offer of assistance). Instead, the two democracies proposed and
established a Non-Intervention treaty in August 1936 that
debarred state and private enterprise in signatory countries from
delivering war material to Spain. Germany and Italy signed the
treaty, though they also continued freely aiding the military rebels.
So Non-Intervention worked solely against the Republic and would
do so for the duration of the war.

When British policy-makers first learned of the military coup, their
preference was for a rapid rebel victory, since this would have
served their two major objectives. The first of these was to prevent a
Spanish war escalating into generalized European conflict. This
risked forcing Britain to fight a war in defence of its imperial
interests on three fronts simultaneously – against Germany, Italy,
and Japan – something that was beyond its military resources and

which therefore had to be avoided at all costs. Secondly, a rebel victory was perceived as the best defence of capital and private property in Spain, including substantial British investment. The popular fervour following the victory of the pro-reform coalition in the elections of February 1936 led some British diplomats and ministers (in what was a predominantly Conservative government) to compare Spain's republican government with Kerensky's in Russia on the eve of the Bolshevik revolution in February 1917. But the two situations were not structurally comparable, and fears of imminent social revolution in Spain (and especially of the nationalization of British assets) were unfounded. In fact, the British establishment's hostility to the Second Republic long pre-dated the 'hot' spring of 1936. It went right back to its birth in April 1931. Britain's governing elite was connected to conservative Spain by class, politics, commerce, and friendship. Its distaste for the Republic's socially reforming agenda was palpable in its snobbish disparagement of Spain's new political class. Soon this hostility could be publicly justified by reference to the anticlerical violence that erupted in some parts of Republican territory in the aftermath of the coup. Political and social prejudice blinded official observers in Britain to the obvious fact: if there had been no military rebellion then there would have been no extra-judicial killing – anticlerical or otherwise. For it was the military coup itself that caused the temporary collapse of public order in Republican Spain. At the same time, the British authorities managed to put a rather different gloss on the killing in the rebel zone. In so far as they acknowledged it at all, it was treated as an unfortunate unpleasantness but one that would have eugenic effects, thus allowing Franco, the 'gentle general', to restore 'order'.

In the week following the coup, Britain obstructed the Republic's defence by refusing its navy the right to refuel in Gibraltar or Tangier. A blind eye was also turned to initial German and Italian intervention. This was decisive since Hitler and Mussolini had their eyes firmly fixed on Britain's reaction. Had it reacted negatively to their initial involvement, then it is clear that the two dictators would not have intervened so lavishly – indeed, might even have ceased their intervention. Neither was yet ready for a confrontation with Britain.

Once the British government was holding aloof, however, then France also reneged on its initial promise to send war material to the Spanish Republic. A sense of vulnerability, increased by the fact that France was now bounded on two sides by fascist powers, made it extremely fearful of diplomatic isolation from Britain. Moreover, the French prime minister, parliamentary socialist Léon Blum, was also acutely aware that hostility to Republican Spain among the more socially conservative sectors of his own new reforming administration could, if he pushed the issue of military aid, shipwreck his chances of enacting social reform in France. Given France's difficulties and the unresponsiveness of Britain, the Spanish Republic had been reduced in August and September to scrambling for arms piecemeal through *ad hoc* purchasing agents – a process as hideously expensive and wasteful as it was inefficient.

The military rebels faced no such difficulties thanks to German and Italian government aid. The largesse of Hitler and Mussolini was, above all, strategically motivated. By supporting the rebels they sought to obliterate the Republic and thus remove the danger of a liberal-left Franco-Spanish bloc that would obstruct their expansionist foreign policy goals. Ideology too played a part. But the anti-communist discourse used by the fascist dictators to justify their intervention in Spain also had an important strategic function. It allowed them to neutralize British opposition to their escalating involvement. The extent to which this strategy went on working throughout the war would surprise even the Nazi and Fascist leaders. They could not understand why Britain chose not to react to their underlying game plan: the weakening of both France and Britain as the dominant imperial powers. For, above all things, Hitler and Mussolini intervened in Spain because they saw it as the most effective way of changing the balance of power in Europe.

By the end of October 1936 the rebels' southern forces were on the outskirts of Madrid. Their arrival had been delayed by a detour in the last week of September to relieve the garrison siege in Toledo. This clinched for General Franco the position of supreme military and political commander in rebel Spain (*Generalísimo*). Franco made the relief of Toledo into a valuable publicity coup, re-enacting it for newsreel cameras that projected to cinema audiences around the world images of the victorious *Generalísimo* touring the rubble. Toledo was also a site of huge symbolic importance to the Spanish Right. In medieval times it had been the first Muslim-controlled city in the Peninsula to be conquered by Christian forces. This gave an added resonance to Franco's decision to divert there – a decision clearly motivated by political considerations, for its military necessity is hard to discern. Indeed, by delaying the advance on Madrid, Franco gave the Republicans vital time to organize the defence of the capital city.

Crucial here was the eleventh-hour provision of military aid by the Soviet Union. Agreed by Stalin in mid-September, the war materiel arrived on the Madrid front just in time to be deployed in the November fighting. Up until this moment the Soviet Union had remained aloof. Moscow ignored an initial plea for aid made by the Republican government back in July – once Madrid realized that France was about to renege. Even so, the plea was made more in desperation than with any real anticipation of success. There were no proper diplomatic channels through which the request for aid could have been pursued. Although the Republic had formally recognized the Soviet Union in June 1933, the first Spanish government ever to do so, there had still been no exchange of diplomatic representatives when the military rose in July 1936.

When the coup happened, the Soviet Union had rapidly backed the British- and French-inspired policy of Non-Intervention. Given the enormous economic, social, and political upheaval occurring inside the Soviet Union, Stalin was as concerned as policy-makers in Britain to keep the international scene in equilibrium. Moreover, since his greatest fear was of an expansionist Nazi Germany, nor had he any desire to alienate Britain by supporting the Spanish Republic. Quite the contrary, by 1936 the Soviet leadership was actively seeking a mutual defence alliance with both Britain and France, a policy Stalin termed 'collective security'. He was convinced that the imperial powers would soon have to understand that the greatest and most urgent threat to their interests lay not in Russian communism but in the territorial ambitions of Nazi Germany. For a time too the Soviet leadership also thought that Non-Intervention, if it could be made to work, would offer the Republic its best chance. Stalin knew that, if the war in Spain escalated, then, in the long term, it would be very difficult for the Republic to compete, even if it could procure foreign armaments, since it was facing rebel forces backed by direct state aid from both Fascist Italy and Nazi Germany, the most sophisticated military-industrial complex of its day.

However, it rapidly became clear that Non-Intervention was not working, and Stalin realized that unless something was done, the Republic was going to collapse under the onslaught. If this happened, then Nazi firepower would be freed up for aggression eastwards – against vulnerable Soviet frontiers. In order to avoid this, Stalin decided to risk British displeasure by dispatching some military assistance. But in an attempt to protect the cherished goal of a defensive alliance with Britain and France, Soviet military assistance to the Republic, unlike its humanitarian equivalent, was never openly acknowledged. The silence of the Soviet press on this matter contrasted with those of Germany and Italy; the Italian press in particular was full of news of 'virile' fascist action in Spain.

Soviet aid saved the Spanish Republic from almost certain military defeat in November 1936. Its tanks and drivers rendered valuable service, as did the small cohort of military and technical advisors, but most important were the Soviet Union's planes and trained pilots, who gave the Republic superiority in the air during the battle for Madrid which thundered on throughout the winter of 1936.

Airpower would rapidly become vital. On those occasions when the Republic had the advantage, it was an important factor in its ability to chalk up rare victories – as it did at Jarama just outside Madrid in February 1937 and at Guadalajara, 50 kilometres northeast of the capital, in March. As a result of these battles, the capital city was held against Franco's armies. The rebels suffered a major defeat and one that turned Madrid into an international symbol of anti-fascist resistance. From across Europe and beyond artists and writers came to participate in the cultural mobilization that formed a vital part of the Republican war effort. They understood that this was the front line in a greater culture war. If fascism won, then it would snuff out the possibility of producing culture freely.

Many anti-fascists also came to Spain to fight. The battle for Madrid involved intense combat and many casualties, nowhere more than among the International Brigades, who were thrown into the breach as the rebel armies reached the capital. The Brigades were composed of volunteer soldiers of the political Left. Some 35,000 would fight for the Spanish Republic between 1936 and 1939 – the strength of the Brigades at any one time being between 12,000 and 16,000 (the higher figure was reached only at the peak of recruitment in spring 1937). The volunteers came from all over the world, but most had their origins in Europe. Even in the two North American contingents from the USA and Canada – some 3,000- and 1,600-strong respectively – the great majority were either European migrants or the children of migrants.

A very high proportion of those who went to fight for Republican Spain (whether from within Europe or beyond) were already political exiles. They came not only from Germany, Italy, and Austria, but from many other European countries also dominated by right-wing nationalist dictatorships, autocratic monarchies, and the radical (fascist) Right – including Hungary, Yugoslavia, Romania, Poland, and Finland. Indeed, it is impossible to understand the International Brigades as an historical phenomenon without taking into account their origins in European

diaspora. The brigaders were part of a mass migration of people –
mainly from the urban working classes – who had already left their
countries of birth at some point after the First World War, either for
economic reasons or to flee political repression, and frequently
both. Among the Canadian volunteers, for example, there were
many Finns who had fled the repression unleashed by the
nationalist leader Mannerheim after the civil war of 1918. One
Canadian Finn even spoke of going to fight in Spain to avenge
his sister who had been killed by the whites (nationalists) during
that war.

In fighting fascism in Spain these exiles and migrants were, then,
taking up unfinished business that went back at least as far as the
1914–18 war. Its dislocations had brutalized politics, inducing the
birth of the anti-democratic nationalisms that had physically
displaced them. For exiles and migrants too, left internationalism
was a form of politics quite naturally reinforced by their own
diasporic condition. It also signified a powerful antidote to the
other, literally murderous, forms of politics inhabiting their own
countries. The stakes were raised further by the economic
depression of the 1930s. Mass unemployment and deprivation –
particularly in urban areas – accelerated political polarization by
seeming to announce the collapse of an untenable capitalist
economy that was still being defended by the forces of the Right.
The brigaders felt that by going to fight the military rebels and their
fascist backers in Spain, they were also striking a blow against
economic and political oppression across the whole continent. They
were thus quite conscious of themselves as political soldiers in an
ongoing European civil war.

This European civil war was, like Spain's own, a culture war too.
Just as the violence of the military rebels targeted the socially,
culturally, and sexually different, so too did the violence being
exercised elsewhere in Europe by the radical Right. This was a form
of politics that everywhere derived from the acute clash between
values and ways of life – rural against urban; tradition against

modernity; fixed social hierarchy against more fluid, egalitarian modes of politics – the same tensions now erupting in Spain.

As a European civil war of culture, it was also a race war. This was not simply about German Nazism; so many of the regimes from which brigader-exiles had fled after 1918 developed forms of politics based on ethnic segregation and 'purification' – aimed both at racial and other minorities. There were many Jewish volunteers among the brigaders – about a quarter of the total. This included quite a high proportion of the Polish brigaders and a specifically Jewish company was formed within the Polish battalion, where it attracted an international membership. This battalion was named after a young Jewish communist, Naftali Botwin, killed in Poland in 1925, its flag bore the words 'for your freedom and ours' in Yiddish and Polish on one side and in Spanish on the other, and members of the Botwin Company would later fight in the French Resistance. Most Jewish brigaders in Spain, however, fought in other units, and many saw their anti-fascism as a more important mark of personal identity than their Jewishness. In fighting fascism in Spain, all the brigaders were resisting many forms of violent social and political exclusion simultaneously. Likewise, those persecuted and incarcerated in the first Nazi camps set up in 1933 were German outsiders, the different, the marginal – whether politically, socially, culturally, or sexually. German international brigaders took to Spain at least one song – *Peat Bog Soldiers* – written by an inmate of the first Nazi camps.

In racial and cultural as well as political terms, then, the heterogeneity of the Brigades made them a living form of opposition to the principles of purification and brutal categorization espoused by facism and, above all, by Nazism. But this was not just about doing battle with European demons.

The Abraham Lincoln Brigade, in which around 90 African Americans fought, was the first non-segregated American military

4. Oliver Law, the black commander of the American Abraham Lincoln Brigade, was killed in action at the battle of Brunete in July 1937. He was the first military commander in US history to lead a unit of troops that was not segregated along racial lines.

unit ever to exist – the United States Army itself continuing to operate segregation throughout the Second World War. Viewed through this optic, what the International Brigades symbolize is a certain spirit of future possibility. They were – though very imperfectly and by no means consciously – the soldiers of cosmopolitan cultural modernity.

It was these egalitarian aspirations that shaped the idea of the Republicans' fight in the Civil War as 'the last great cause', as the front line in the fight for a more equal and inclusive form of politics in Europe and beyond. The survival of this idea long after Republican defeat was made possible not least by the extraordinarily intense quality of the comradeship and solidarity that so many of the foreign volunteers – whether soldiers or medical personnel – experienced in Spain and took away with them as an incandescent and life-changing memory. The poet Edwin Rolfe, who was with the Lincolns in Spain, expressed it thus as he later trained to fight in the World War:

I am eager to enter it, eager to end it.
Perhaps this will be the last one.
[. . . . . . .]
But my heart is forever captive of that other war
that taught me first the meaning of peace and of comradeship
and always I think of my friend who amid the apparition of bombs
saw on the lyric lake the single perfect swan.

('First Love', 1943)

Precisely because they were used as the Republic's shock troops, the Brigades sustained very high casualties, especially in the early stages of the war. The British contingent was decimated at the battle of Jarama in February 1937, where the Lincolns too sustained savage losses. Nor was there, at the beginning, much experience in Spain of how to deal with battlefield death and injury on such a scale. The learning curve was almost perpendicular. Crucial assistance came in the form of foreign medical volunteers: doctors and nurses whose support, along with fund-raising for humanitarian and medical supplies, was an integral part of progressive and left-wing solidarity with the Republic at war. But the benefits proved more than reciprocal: out of this collaboration came advances in the emergency treatment of casualties – particularly in triage and blood transfusion techniques – which would be of major benefit in the World War that followed.

There were other kinds of advances too – although here the balance sheet was more ambiguous. Salaria Kea, a nurse with the American medical bureau, and Thyra Edwards, a social worker who helped with the refugee Children's Colonies set up by the Republican government, were both African American women who served in Spain – the only two to do so. But when another young woman, Evelyn Hutchins, applied to be sent as an ambulance driver, she came up against entrenched prejudice. The political Left, though keen to further racial equality, could only conceive of recruiting women to Spain as nurses or support staff. In the end Hutchins won, but hers was an isolated victory. Women were not generally recruited for volunteer service in Republican Spain except in functions considered appropriate to the mainstream, and thus socially conservative, gender norms of the times. The experience and memory of this would, after 1945, lead women in the American communist movement to challenge the party's stance on gender. This contributed to a broader debate that, in turn, helped produce the more culturally aware New Left movement of the 1960s. The 'good fight', as the American brigaders named the struggle to save the Spanish Republic, was, then, about more than one kind of fight.

The organizational axis of the International Brigades was from the start provided by the European communist movement. In the 1930s this movement offered by far the most active and dynamic form of organized opposition to fascism, and thus attracted huge swathes of left and liberal constituencies to participate. Nowhere was this more in evidence than over solidarity with Republican Spain. Communist organizations were at the forefront of the campaign to get Non-Intervention lifted. Their pre-eminence here was also a function of the ambiguous position of European social democracy, whose political parties and trade unions were still much influenced by currents of anti-war and pacifist sentiment deriving from the experience of 1914–18. This initially led many of them to support the policy of Non-Intervention, and even after it was seen to be damaging the Republic, socialist leaderships in Europe remained generally reluctant to challenge their governments over the legality of Non-Intervention.

The human raw material for the Brigades was rapidly channelled by the Communist International (Comintern) mainly under the auspices of the French Communist Party (PCF), which also provided the single largest national contingent of the Brigades – more than 9,000 volunteers across the war. The event that galvanized the Comintern into action on recruitment was clearly the Soviet Union's decision in September 1936 to provide some military assistance to the Republic.

The International Brigades were, then, an element in Stalin's reactive emergency planning. The Comintern provided the vital organizational mechanism that would make it possible systematically to channel to Spain the military expertise of the international Left in order to stave off Republican defeat in the autumn of 1936. Parlous though the military state of the Republic was at that stage, the government proved a difficult interlocutor in the negotiations that brought the International Brigades into existence in October 1936. The Republican military command and most army officers serving with the Republic were hostile to the Brigades both for reasons of chauvinism and professional pride. As soon as the rebuilding of an integrated Republican army was under way in 1937, it began to exert an ineluctable force of attraction that saw the Brigades incorporated to its ranks by autumn of that year. This process also meant that the Brigades, though they retained their numerical identities, were less and less 'foreign' as the war went on. For there was a concerted policy of topping them up with Spanish conscripts – a process that accelerated as brigader recruitment declined from its peak in the early months of 1937.

For all of these reasons, it is a mistake to reduce the complex historical phenomenon of the International Brigades to the simplistic schema of a Comintern army. Stalin could not order European nationals to fight for the Spanish Republic in the same way that Hitler or Mussolini could (and did) conscript Germans and Italians. The international brigaders who went to Spain were volunteers, and as the sociological and historical background already sketched indicates, their motives were as complex and rooted in personal experience as those of the very early volunteers for the Republic (in July and August 1936) who had gone to Spain in an entirely individual capacity. Once there, all volunteers came to be subject to military discipline. If this had not happened, then they would have been useless to the Republic, but for some – even for a minority in the Brigades – this rankled precisely because they had signed up as volunteers. No doubt this sense of disillusion was also a function of their shocked realization of how unprepared they were to face the harsh conditions of warfare in Spain – especially given the antiquated weaponry they were obliged to use, courtesy of Non-Intervention.

Given that the main function of Comintern personnel was to ensure discipline in the Brigades, there were plenty of material causes for clashes even without taking into account the excessively rigid and doctrinaire organizational and political culture that operated inside the Comintern. This rigidity would grow across the war, at least in part as a response to the Comintern's inevitably quite limited ability to affect military outcomes in Spain. In other words, the zeal or 'political correctness' of many Comintern rapporteurs was often intended as a defence against possible charges of technical and organizational incompetence being levelled either by their own executive body or by the Soviet leadership. Rigidity was, in short, an indication of Comintern weakness, not strength.

In the autumn and winter of 1936 the war entered not just the physical space that was Madrid or the minds of those soldiers – Spanish or otherwise – fighting on the central front, but also the consciousness of the city's civilian population. This first occurred through the experience of aerial bombing. It was on 28 August that the population of Madrid suffered their first air raids – indeed the first of their kind to occur anywhere in Europe. The bombing itself and the requisite need to organize civil defence began to forge a new sense of a Republican community in adversity. In 1936 this was specific to the Madrid area; over the next two years the war would arrive successively in different parts of Republican territory. In this way, gradually, forms of Republican identity began to coalesce as a result of the war itself – whether experienced on the home front or at the front line.

Violent deaths occasioned by the conflict, but especially those in battle, also made the 'meaning' of the war for both sides. In the case

5. A shop window display in Republican Spain (Valencia, October 1937) which indicates how key political symbols – the incarnation of the Second Republic as a pretty young woman (*la niña bonita*) – and iconic figures like the anarchist leader Buenaventura Durruti, killed in November 1936 on the Madrid front, had been incorporated into popular culture.

of Francoist identities, these could be more easily consolidated after 1939, while Republican ones, shattered by defeat, would thereafter be confined to private and subterranean spaces. The extreme time compression in the emergence of wartime Republican identities makes them appear ultra-contingent, subjective, and fragile. But we should be wary of viewing them as any less real for that than other forms of national identity.

The war was also borne – first to Madrid, but then beyond – by refugees. The first major influx came from the south in the summer of 1936, fleeing ahead of Franco's African army. They passed through Madrid in the autumn and, swelled by more refugees from the besieged capital, this human tide flowed on to Barcelona and Valencia – cities where the war was still a distant rumour. The refugees also constituted a form of accelerated population mobility, and thus a form of social change. In addition to the specific traumas of wartime displacement, the sudden transplantation of the southern poor to the more economically and culturally developed milieux of northeast Spain inflicted a severe culture shock. While those most severely affected were the refugees themselves, this shock also had a reciprocal dimension, as indicated in Quaker relief work reports from Barcelona and Valencia. One, written in May 1937, describes the refugees from the southern city of Málaga as 'wild', 'half Moors', and terrified of 'lists' for fear of what their exposure to state or public authorities might mean.

As the rebel army dug in to besiege Madrid's perimeter, the conflict turned into a long war of attrition against the Republic. Hitler and Mussolini recognized rebel Spain in November 1936. But the epic battles around Madrid proved to them – and in particular to Mussolini – that only a massive escalation of German and Italian aid could ensure Franco's victory. Hitler encouraged Mussolini to take the strain. He did so to such an extent that it would damage Italy's military effectiveness in the World War. German aid to Franco also increased, but it was qualitatively concentrated on armament technology, equipment, and airpower. Such was the scale of Mussolini's aid in weaponry and manpower (75,000 troops), we can say that from March 1937 Fascist Italy was at war with the Spanish Republic.

The escalation of the war and the manifest military and diplomatic advantages rapidly accruing to the rebels also produced profound political changes inside Republican Spain. The race was on to build the state and a modern war machine – the only way the Republic could now resist the military enemy. The greatest challenge was to reconstruct an army. The coup had shattered army unity and the Republican command had to begin almost from scratch. There were excruciating material dislocations and shortages, massively exacerbated by the impact of Non-Intervention. Political opposition to militarization among militia fighters was not so much of an issue where they had already experienced action against Franco's forces, as on the central fronts around Madrid. A much more serious problem was the militia's abiding distrust of professional army officers – itself scarcely surprising in the light of the coup.

This distrust made the new post of political commissar crucial. The commissars were appointed by all Republican political organizations and their job was to explain the rationale of military orders, to look after the practical welfare of their troops, and remind them of the *raison d'être* of the war. The professional officers who remained loyal to the Republic were often (though not always) contemptuous of the untrained militia, and this rigid, closed mentality meant that in the early months they frequently failed to make the best use of them.

Crucial time for military reorganization was also lost in the winter of 1936 because those in political charge of the Republic did not understand quickly enough the nature of the war they were being called upon to fight. Political tensions between centre and periphery also caused further hold-ups when they could least be afforded. Even half-hearted attempts to increase centralized control of wartime planning and resources led to debilitating clashes between the central Republican government and the newly emergent Basque regional authority in the north. It was controlled by the Basque nationalist party (PNV) which sought sovereign rights, opposing all attempts to bring Basque industry or the militarized Basque fighting units under central Republican control. By the time a tougher new Republican government emerged that was ready to force the issue, the Basque front was already under major attack from Franco's forces. It would fall in the summer of 1937, depriving the Republic of crucial heavy industrial resources and thereby significantly reducing its chances of winning the war outright militarily.

The collapse of the Basque front occurred just as Republican military reorganization was beginning to cohere. The battle of Brunete, fought on the outskirts of Madrid in July 1937, and probably the bloodiest single battle of the war, was the defining moment: the birth in fire of the new Republican army. Even then, though, its effectiveness was ominously constrained by Non-Intervention-provoked hold-ups of war materiel on the French frontier. By late summer the Republican army was also well on the way to establishing an entire corps dedicated to innovative forms of guerrilla warfare behind rebel lines. Although this was mainly composed of Spanish soldiers, a contingent of international brigaders also fought in the guerrilla from its inception in early 1937. Many of them were of Finnish origin, including Canadian Finns and one Finnish-American, Bill Aalto. He was a 22-year-old working-class boy from the Bronx who became a captain in the guerrilla and later, in 1938, participated in an important commando raid that constitutes the only operation of its kind ever undertaken by the Spanish army (see Chapter 5). A few years later, Aalto's comrade-in-arms and fellow participant in that commando action, Irv Goff, would have an opportunity to re-use the skills learned in Spain when during the World War he was parachuted back into occupied Europe by US special services to take part in the irregular war of resistance behind the lines – the only kind of active service for which the American government did not actively discriminate against those of its citizens who had fought for the Spanish Republic.

The imperative of war also saw the acceleration of a process of mass mobilization on the Republican home front – especially of women and young people – whose origins went back to the pre-war period and which, in turn, constituted a form of social and political modernization. Women were recruited *en masse* to industrial war work. This involved practical training that improved their

6. The political mobilization of young people in Republican Spain was also part of a broader process of social and cultural change

7. *Miliciana* (militia woman) **in Madrid at the beginning of the war**

educational level. Even more significantly, it constituted exposure to cultural alternatives that carried within them the potential for a transformation in gender relations – one of many new cultural potentials that perished with defeat.

The Republican war worker (Figure 8) was the real face of the 'new woman' in 1930s Spain. The more familiar – even clichéd – image of the blue-overalled *miliciana* (Figure 7) is more problematic. There were some women militia fighters, and women also participated in undercover forms of fighting, including in the guerrilla – usually in highly dangerous liaison roles. But most of the photographs of militia women that we possess do not bear witness to either of these harsh realities; they were almost all taken in the early days of the conflict and carry the unmistakeable stamp of 'war as fiesta'. They are highly choreographed images, designed to maximize the

8. Republican woman war worker

decorative effect of their female subjects. Just like the famous posters of the *milicianas*, they were aimed predominantly at a male audience and, in the case of the posters, were actively intended as a recruitment device to persuade that male audience to volunteer for military service.

9. A literacy class for Republican soldiers

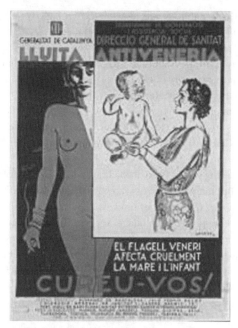

10. Republican health education poster, with misogynistic subtext, warning of the dangers posed by venereal disease to the health of mother and child

Republican mobilization, like other modern war mobilization, was about both practical and psychological conscription, and thus it became an important agent of social and cultural change. By the latter part of 1937, conscription was making a significant impact.

In order to build the Republican army, large numbers of young men were taken out of a rural milieu to be trained. This also involved developing basic literacy, numeracy, and public health campaigns. In a country like Spain, with very low levels of education among its rural majority, these too were crucial components in the process of nation-building. Once again, the role of the political commissars was a crucial one. Out of the intense experience of the front line – combat, comradeship, and common suffering – there would emerge a specifically Republican consciousness among many combatants who had had no pre-war political affiliations.

Another factor in the Republic's success in reaching people was in its impressive repertory of innovative propaganda techniques (see Figure 11). In particular, Republican cultural mobilization saw the launching of photomontage as a weapon of war. Material was provided by leading figures of the European avant-garde – notably the exiled German artist John Heartfield, who made the famous montage *They Shall Not Pass*, which shows Fascist and Nazi vultures preying on the Madrid skyline, held at bay by anti-fascist bayonets. But many Spaniards were also making innovative war art, including a strong element of modernist photomontage – as, for example, in the poster and collage work of the Valencian artist Josep Renau. (During the war Renau was also Director of Fine Arts, an important post with responsibility for protecting national artistic treasures from bomb damage.) Photomontage is one format that clearly distinguishes Republican wartime art from what was produced in the Francoist zone. Both had artists and propagandists

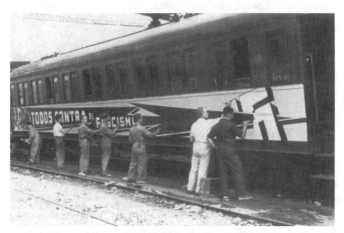

11. **Republican propaganda train being painted with anti-fascist insignia**

12. Wall poem in Madrid, autumn 1937, commemorating the
Republican forces in the north (Asturias)

who worked in a figurative tradition and both also used mechanized, modernist images of the human form to conjure 'brave new orders' (the heroic soldier in the famous Republican literacy poster could be a fascist image – although the caption clarifies that it is not). But photomontage was one modernist technique that Francoist production could not incorporate, as it had strong internationalist and cosmopolitan connotations. The brash contrasts in photomontage broke the rules of formal composition, and made a virtue of immediacy and contingency. As a form it was also geared towards mechanical reproduction. This was exactly what the right had in mind when it spoke of 'degeneracy' and 'cultural bolshevism'.

Cultural bolshevism

'Cultural bolshevism', a term coined by the Nazis, was used to denounce modernist, non-representational, and avant-garde cultural production, which the Right in Europe saw as eroding political hierarchy and contaminating national cultural traditions. In Nazi Germany an exhibition of modern art was mounted under the title 'degenerate art'. The idea that culture or society might 'degenerate', as if it were a biological organism, had considerable currency in 20th-century social and political thought of the inter-war period – especially, but not exclusively, among conservative sectors. It can be traced in part to the work of 19th-century scientists, including Charles Darwin's on the evolution of species, which had encouraged the idea that biological laws could be applied to society (social Darwinism). In Spain many of the same ideas would develop from 'regenerationist' thought, which emerged after the loss of empire in 1898.

But in spite of the substantively different cultural values and political ideologies underpinning Republican and Francoist Spain, the war saw the common continuation and acceleration of a process of social change. The vast expansion of the (fascist) Falange and Spanish Communist Party organizations fulfilled comparable functions in the two zones, incorporating previously unmobilized sectors of the population (and especially women and young people) to the war effort and, thus, to the state or public sphere. One factor in the appeal of the Spanish communist movement to many highly disparate social constituencies in wartime Republican Spain was the increased popularity of the Soviet Union. As the only major country to break through the international isolation stifling the Republic, it had provided a tremendous boost to popular morale. There was a widespread feeling of optimism that here was a powerful country whose dynamic support could enable the Republicans to win the war. Hence for a time the commemorative ceremonies, rhetoric, and iconography celebrating Soviet solidarity with the Republic found a popular response. The Soviet Union became 'flavour of the month'. In Madrid in the winter of 1936–7 there was a craze for Russian hats and insignia of all kinds. Women's magazines also featured Russian hairstyles and fashion as the last word in chic (see Figure 13).

But this generalized attraction and the superficial décor that accompanied it had little to do with Marxist-Leninism, or indeed political ideology of any kind. So it makes little sense to talk as some commentators have of Republican politics and society becoming 'Sovietized'. Rather, the popular mood had fastened onto the Soviet Union in quite a different way, as an icon of modernity. This had a certain precedent in the 1920s in Spain when forward-thinking, though not necessarily politically minded, urban constituencies were already associating the Soviet Union with technological and cultural modernity. This was not dissimilar to the way that many post-war constituencies in Spain would project onto North American products and images their own aspirations to progress and development – as depicted in Luis Berlanga's 1953 film

LA MODA EN MOSCU

Vestido combinado en seda marrón con cuerpo en crêpe de china a rayas de colores marrón, amarillo y blanco.
Modelo dibujado por Makarova y confeccionado en la Casa de los Modelos, de Moscú.

Tailleur en seda blanca con chaleco de rayas blancas y azul claro, y cinturón azul oscuro dibujado por Moukhara.

Vestido de verano en seda blanca, con chaleco rojo vivo en crêpe de china, y guarniciones rojo oscuro salpicadas en blanco, según modelo dibujado por Soudaké-vitch.

13. High fashion from Moscow: a plate from a women's magazine in wartime Madrid

Bienvenido Mr Marshall. For a 21st-century reader in the West, that may seem a counter-intuitive comparison, but clearly the perceptions of Spaniards in the 1920s and 1930s were not filtered through the Cold War. This construction of both the Soviet Union and the USA shared a common element: the dearth of national, that is Spanish, models on which to draw, although, precisely because of Republican defeat, this lack was undoubtedly far more acute in the 1950s and 1960s than it had been in the 1920s and 1930s.

The wartime race to build the Republican state also produced a central government drive against all manifestations of the localism that had emerged in the wake of the military rising – from village committees through regional councils (such as the famous Council of Aragon) to the Catalan regional government itself. In part, this was also a drive against radical sectors of the left that had championed the collectivized and cooperative forms of agriculture and industry that mushroomed in the wake of the coup. Those ranged against the radical Left were not only communists, but also large swathes of the socialist parliamentary party and its trade union, assorted republican parties, and even some sectors of the anarcho-syndicalist CNT. And, of course, it wasn't just a question of these political entities themselves, but also of entire social constituencies within Republican society that each represented. This alliance was an attempt to re-establish the broad, reforming liberal democratic coalition of workers and middle-class sectors first created with the birth of the Republic in 1931. It had been revived after the electoral victory of February 1936, but was then disrupted by the military coup in July. The victory of this broad alliance was symbolically sealed in May 1937 when Republican 'law and order' triumphed over the social and political protests of radicalized workers and the urban poor in the streets of Barcelona. These were the famous 'May Days'. As a result, a new wartime government was appointed under the parliamentary socialist Juan Negrín.

There were many reasons why street fighting erupted in Barcelona.

Many more reasons, indeed, than met the eye of the events' most famous chronicler, George Orwell, who, it should be borne in mind, read neither Spanish nor Catalan. In *Homage to Catalonia*, he rightly identified the fighting as having to do with conflicting models of how to organize Republican society and politics. But he exaggerates the role played by both Catalan and Spanish communists. Untenable too is his conspiracy theory – that the May Days were somehow deliberately provoked. In fact, social and political tensions had been building up in the city since the beginning of 1937. The Catalan government, of which the communists were a part, but only a part, had gradually been restoring to itself the executive powers it had lost to workers and trade union committees in the aftermath of the military coup.

Part of this process saw the government re-introduce market forces to food supply in the city. The net effect was to penalize the poorest urban constituencies, the people who had been at the sharp end of Republican budgetary stringency and public order policy since 1931 (see Chapter 1). Their fragile economies were also the ones most dislocated by the effects of the war – which in Catalonia especially included severe sectoral unemployment. The poor could not afford the black market, nor could they access the burgeoning barter economy, for they were often urban migrants from other areas of Spain who thus had no contacts in the Catalan countryside. With the re-introduction of a free market, they lost the safety net of the CNT's supply committees, which had been the major instrument provisioning the urban poor of Barcelona throughout the first months of the war. Inflation was also rampant in spite of official price controls.

By the end of 1936, there were nearly 350,000 refugees as well as thousands of unofficially displaced persons in Catalonia. Together, they increased the total population by well over 10%. The extra pressure on housing and food was greatest in the poorest inner-city areas where the inadequacies of a rudimentary rationing system created a subsistence crisis that provoked street protests during the early months of 1937. Nor do the displays of tinned food Orwell spotted in grocers' windows gainsay this. These were luxury products and could play no role in mitigating the food crisis – or at least not given the government's enforcement of free market rules. As before the war, there were familiar scenes of the police breaking up food protests and protecting commercial premises from popular requisition.

On top of this economic distress came the hostile political action of the Catalan government. If we add to this potent mix the radical traditions of direct action prevalent among the urban constituencies of 'red' Barcelona, historically articulated by the CNT, then the explosion of street fighting in May 1937 becomes entirely explicable. What sparked it was the police bid to eject the worker committee from Barcelona's central telephone exchange. But the force of the explosion derived from the action simultaneously being undertaken by police across the city to regain control of public order by disarming the workers' patrols that had been established in the aftermath of the military coup.

Once the streets had exploded, then many sectarian political struggles were pursued to deadly effect. Spanish and Catalan communists colluded with representatives of the Comintern, most notoriously in the murder of Andreu Nin, the leader of the Catalan-based dissident communist party POUM. Nin, who had lived in Moscow in the 1920s, was part of the Bolshevik inner circle and had once been Trotsky's secretary. The POUM leader was detained in a clandestine party prison. Illegal prisons, or *checas*, originally appeared in Republican territory in the chaotic aftermath of the military rising in July 1936. Faced with the coup-induced collapse of public order, left political parties, unions, and militia committees all established their own detention centres. But the *checas* had been eradicated as the Republican authorities regained political control; indeed, their eradication was crucial to the constitutional credibility of the government. So their recrudescence in May 1937 was a serious blow. The scandal of illegal detentions and killings such as Nin's intensified the already considerable anxieties over public order provoked by the street fighting, and thus contributed to the mounting pressure for cabinet change and for the implementation by government of more rigorous surveillance and security measures.

The fact that Soviet intelligence personnel were also involved in some of the shady activities during the May Days has led some commentators to exaggerate the degree of political influence exercised by the Soviet Union in the Republican zone. So it is worthwhile remembering that in the major cities of wartime Spain there were to be found intelligence agents from all the major powers. This is scarcely surprising given that the Spanish Civil War was universally agreed to be the neuralgic point of international politics and diplomacy.

There was certainly a good deal of suspicion driving Soviet intelligence activity – not least because of the climate of fear produced by the political turmoil inside the Soviet Union, and also because Soviet personnel had a tendency to project the fears inherited from the Russian Civil War onto the Spanish situation, seeing saboteurs and internal enemies everywhere. But these were not always unreasonable fears – Spain's was, after all, a civil war – and Republican intelligence itself did successfully dismantle a Francoist intelligence network in Barcelona at the time of the May Days. Nor was the Soviet Union the only power involved in political assassinations in Spain. The Italian secret police, Mussolini's OVRA (*Opera per la Vigilanza e la Repressione Antifascista*), were almost certainly responsible for the assassination of leading Italian anarchist Camillo Berneri and his secretary Francesco Barbieri during the May events in Barcelona. A month later, the OVRA also killed two other leading Italian anti-fascist exiles in France – the brothers Carlo and Nello Rosselli. Yet no one has ever suggested that because the Italian regime was able to carry out this assassination it had undue influence over the French government.

Not all the sectarian violence during the May Days was the result of tensions in the international communist movement, nor indeed was it authored by the Spanish communists. In the pre-war Republic, many of the conflicts between organizations of the Left had played out violently. The coming of the war did not wipe out the memory of these disputes. Indeed, as they mainly concerned issues of political influence, clientele and membership rivalries, the wartime situation intensified such clashes in Republican Spain. Once the May street fighting erupted in Barcelona, it precipitated a quantity of bloodletting on all sides. Clashes occurred between members of the CNT and the socialist-led trade union, UGT; between socialists and communists, and between the rival branches of Catalan communism – as the ghosts of decades of labour wars and political infighting stalked the streets and meeting rooms of the city.

The Republican government also imprisoned many members of the CNT and POUM in Catalonia in the aftermath of May. Its aim was to restore war discipline and ensure that such events could never occur again. The POUM's leaders were arrested for having publicly defended in newspaper editorials those who had rebelled on the streets. It is highly significant that the POUM arrests were made in June as Bilbao, the industrial powerhouse of the north, fell to Franco's forces. The POUM leaders were charged with treasonous rebellion against the wartime government and imprisoned pending trial.

But the outcome of the May crisis and the appointment of a new government was not just about disciplining the radical and collectivist left. What marked the Negrín cabinet out from preceding ones was its grasp of international politics and diplomacy, and also its crucial understanding that a wartime outcome favourable to the Republic would depend upon actively changing the stance of France and Britain. Over the next 18 months Negrín would take personal charge of Republican diplomacy in a desperate attempt to turn the international situation around. The Republic, in the meanwhile, steeled itself for all-out military resistance.

Chapter 4
The making of rebel Spain

You may conquer [*vencer*] but you will never convince [*convencer*]. This will be the victory of the worst, of a brand of Catholicism that is not Christian and of a paranoid militarism bred in the colonial campaigns.

(Miguel de Unamuno)

Anger has its roots in fear.

It is usual for those writing on the Spanish Civil War to draw a sharp contrast between the political unity of the rebels under Franco and the fragmentation and discord of the Republicans, but the reasons for this are rarely well explained. Certainly there existed a much higher degree of ideological commonality among those supporting the rebels. The great fear felt by all pro-Francoist sectors, and which underlay the anger directed at everything 'Republican', provided a tremendous force for political and psychological cohesion. But after May 1937, disunity in Republican Spain had rather less to do with ideology and internal politics than it did with the cumulatively negative material and psychological impact of Non-Intervention, military defeat, and the Republic's rapidly deteriorating position internationally. If Franco's armies had not been steadily advancing and (almost always) winning, courtesy of their German and Italian backers, then there would have been much greater political stresses and strains within the wartime Francoist coalition too. The democratic ethos underpinning the Republican polity – even if curtailed by wartime imperatives – meant that political disagreements and divisions were also much more visible, while the rebel unity forged from the fragmentation of July 1936 was at least in part the appearance of unity produced by dictatorial techniques. This chapter will explore how rebel Spain was built – 'top-down' and 'bottom-up' – while also analysing the evolving international dimension of the war.

The title of this chapter refers to 'rebel' rather than 'Francoist' Spain not because there can be any dispute about the rapid rise to military and political pre-eminence of General Francisco Franco, but rather to remind us that this ascent was a process not a *fait accompli*. Franco and his closest supporters worked very hard to consolidate and extend his personal power. Later, part of this work would involve elaborating propaganda that presented Franco as the 'man of destiny', divinely pre-ordained for power. Franco himself almost certainly came to believe his own myth. But there is no reason why we should.

Franco's rise, though not irresistible, was greatly assisted by a number of fortuitous deaths. These saw the removal of his most serious rivals – either through accident or Republican execution. But Franco's greatest advantage at the start of the war was his control of the Army of Africa. Linked to this was the fact that it was Franco's personal initiative that had done most to galvanize Hitler and Mussolini into action on behalf of the rebels. The Germans and Italians saw the Spanish Right as a collection of endlessly conspiring groupuscules, poorly coordinated and of limited vision. Nor, initially at least, were they impressed by General Mola, the director of the conspiracy – partly because his request for foreign aid was modest and partly because he made it through monarchist representatives who were counted among the ineffective groupuscules. But in Franco both Hitler and Mussolini saw a serious operator with a strategic plan, and this contributed rapidly to the emergence of Franco as the 'name'. On the day of the military coup, the British press had referred to him as the brother of the more famous aviator, Ramón Franco. A bare week later both London and Rome were already calling the rebels 'Franco's forces' (*i franchisti*). Franco had substantial advantages, but he also worked very hard to make the most of them. As soon as the coup occurred he set up his own press office – which speaks volumes both for his ambition and his self-belief. The press office also allowed Franco to extract the maximum propaganda and political advantage from the liberation of the Toledo garrison at the end of September (discussed in Chapter 3).

Franco, fresh from his victorious campaign in the south, had already taken over as supreme military and political chief of the rebel forces. Via fellow generals who had connections to the monarchists and the fascist Falange, Franco managed to persuade both groups that he would further their aims. Indeed, the fact that Franco did not identify with any particular political organization recommended him equally to civilian and military rightists. Only one of his fellow conspirators, the senior officer General Miguel Cabanellas, opposed Franco's appointment at the meeting of the military junta in Salamanca on 21 September 1936. Cabanellas, the junta's symbolic president and an *Africanista* who had once commanded Franco, declared prophetically that if they gave Spain to Franco, he would think it belonged to him, and if they gave him absolute power he would never relinquish it.

While Franco did not have specific political affiliations – other than an ill-defined monarchism that he held in common with most of the officer corps – it was nonetheless evident from the beginning that Franco's war aims were political in a more fundamental way. As we have already seen in Chapter 2, his military strategy was shaped from the very beginning by his mission to 'save Spain' – or rather to preserve a certain kind of social and political order inside the geographical space of Spain. So much about how Franco saw himself in relation to the world derived from his experience in the colonial campaigns in North Africa. His unshakeable self-belief and stubbornness – whether in military or political matters – owed more than a little to the *Africanista* officer's generic territorial tenacity. Nor was Cabanellas the only one to perceive this; a senior Republican officer, once himself an *Africanista*, also later remarked:

> we are told, 'Take so many men, occupy such-and-such a position and do not move from there until you get further orders.' The position occupied by Franco is the nation and since he has no superior officer, he will not move from there.

Secure in his beliefs, Franco had no doubt that he was justified in using terror against the civilian population. He opened cities and towns to mass aerial bombing. Spain was the first European country to suffer this acme of modern warfare. The bombing was achieved courtesy of Franco's German and Italian fascist backers, but it was unthinkable without his explicit approval. After Madrid and Durango came the attack on Guernica, the symbolic seat of Basque nationalism. The town, which had no anti-aircraft defences, was annihilated on 26 April 1937 in three hours of saturation bombing carried out by the German Condor Legion and the Italian Aviazione Legionaria. The key strategic target in the attack was not a military one, but rather civilian morale. Guernica was intended to kill the Basque appetite for resistance, and in an important sense it did achieve this.

Some 15,000 children were evacuated to avoid the bombing. They were sent to various destinations, including Britain, which had historic and trading ties to the Basque Country; 5,000 children went to Belgium, and a further 3,000 to the Soviet Union. But what was intended as a temporary respite would for many become the odyssey of a lifetime, and even those who attempted the return would experience the exile's perpetual estrangement of culture and identity.

Most big Republican centres of population were bombed.

14. An anti-German propaganda poster produced by the anarcho-syndicalist CNT showing the effects of mass bombing on Republican cities (here Madrid). Its ironic use of the word 'ikultur!' is an implicit rejoinder to Franco's claim to be fighting in defence of civilization.

Barcelona, with poor air defences, would suffer successive waves of raids between January and May 1938. But although the air raids caused great panic and left much suffering and destruction in their wake, the feelings they provoked tended to be ones of hatred and resentment rather than fear. Albeit in a negative way, the bombs Franco sent also played their part in creating a new sense of Republican identity among broad sectors of Spain's urban population.

What has remained particularly shocking about the air raids to outside observers is that they were occurring in a civil war – Franco was doing it to his 'own' people. But of course this was not the *Generalísimo*'s perception, nor that of his closest comrades-in-arms; theirs was a higher purpose: the purification of 'Spain'. Achieving this demanded not just a colonial war against the insubordinate poor of the deep south, industrial cities too were seen as a major source of moral pollution. General Mola, who, until his demise in a plane crash in June 1937, was even more vehement about this than Franco, spoke of razing the industry of Bilbao and Barcelona – only in this way could Spain be purged of what was most poisoning it. In other words, the health of the 'nation' required the elimination of the industrial proletariat.

Notwithstanding the spectacular violence of mass aerial bombardment, summer 1937 saw a marked change of pace in Francoist war strategy. After the war of rapidly advancing militia columns in the first months, it now became a *guerra de desgaste* – a war of attrition. Franco was not an imaginative or innovative strategist, but he did not need to be given the kind of war he envisaged. More than any other rebel commander, Franco understood that the war had to be long and arduous. He actively wanted it to be so – for otherwise his fundamental objective, to prostrate the political enemy, could not be achieved. It thus became a war to control people rather than just territory. Franco said as much in April 1937 to the Italian ambassador, Roberto Cantalupo, when he explained that the Italians' preferred strategy of rapid military conquest would be a huge mistake in a civil war since this would not tackle the real question of how to 'redeem' the conquered territory.

> The work of pacification and moral redemption must necessarily be undertaken slowly and methodically, otherwise military occupation will serve no purpose.

In the pursuit of this quite specific goal, Franco was prepared to incur huge losses among his own troops that a different kind of war could have avoided. Hence the reminder by one Spanish army officer that Franco himself was responsible for the deaths of more Francoists than anyone else – by his very choice of a strategy of *desgaste*.

Franco's conviction was total that the Army had an absolute right to impose its will on Spanish society and that military organization was the best means of structuring that society. Franco, like so many of the officers who had masterminded the coup, subscribed fully to the idea of a squad of soldiers 'saving civilization'. But he also understood the necessity of what his closest collaborators advised. The initial 'battlefield state' (*estado campamental*) had to evolve if his victory was to be the lasting political one he sought. The brains behind the creation of both a formal state structure and a Francoist mass movement was Ramón Serrano Suñer, a brilliant lawyer who had been active in the quasi-fascist youth movement of Spain's mass Catholic party, CEDA. He was also a lifelong friend of José Antonio Primo de Rivera, the leader of the Falange executed in a Republican gaol in November 1936. Serrano Suñer had one other major advantage: he was *Generalísimo* Franco's brother-in-law (*cuñado*), and was soon nicknamed by sharp political tongues the *cuñadísimo* (chief brother-in-law).

Serrano Suñer, the architect of the new Francoist state and soon to be the most powerful figure in rebel Spain after Franco, had almost been a victim of the extra-judicial killing in the Republican zone which claimed the lives of his two brothers. There was then a strong personal charge reinforcing Serrano Suñer's political hostility to Republican democracy. (He would later bear a high degree of personal political responsibility in the decision to allow the deportation of Spanish Republicans to Nazi concentration camps in 1940.) Not only did Serrano Suñer's undoubted intellectual capacity recommend him to Franco, so too did his lack of a personal power base – which meant he could never challenge the *Generalísimo*'s own. He worked alongside Franco's brother and secretary, Nicolás. In April 1937 they brought about the unification of the Falange and the Carlist monarchists whose militias also composed the two most numerous elements in the new mass army then under construction.

The unification was a shotgun marriage whose chief beneficiary was Franco. At a stroke he gained a bureaucracy and a political support base, while also bringing his main rivals under his direct control. Some old guard Falangists ('old shirts') who opposed the unification on ideological grounds were excluded from the new unified organization, or 'Movement' (*el Movimiento*) as it was known. But new recruits flooded in. These 'new shirts' joined for the jobs and career opportunities it offered, rather in the way that large numbers of people had also joined the Fascist Party in Italy after Mussolini came to power. The patronage Franco disbursed helped him to consolidate his own power by diluting, if not entirely neutralizing, the old guard's opposition. This would erupt again after the war – as would the tensions between the Falange, the monarchists, and those connected with the organizational networks of the Catholic Church, as competing elements in Franco's power base. Many old shirt Falangists joined the Blue Division, which Franco sent to fight with the German armies on the Eastern Front in 1941 – thereby also offloading a potentially troublesome source of domestic opposition. There would also be post-war conflicts between the Falange and the military cupola. But the Falange was never strong enough to pose a serious challenge here because the ever-cautious Franco saw to it during the war that no politically homogenous military units could cohere within his new mass army. Likewise, post-war attempts by the Falange to exert control through specific army sections such as the parachute division were blocked, and 'political' generals in the higher echelons of power who became involved in such plots were severely disciplined by Franco.

For the duration of the Civil War, however, those inside the Francoist camp whose political ambitions had been disappointed, or who were otherwise critical, held themselves in check. The fact that their army was almost always winning helped enormously here. So too did a strong sense of shared purpose – rooted in the loathing all Francoists felt for the Republic and their determination to eradicate the political and cultural challenge of 'disordered modernity' that it posed to their own preferred world of 'natural' order and hierarchy.

Real social and cultural developments in the rebel zone, however, indicate a rather more complex and ambiguous situation than the idealized binary vision cherished by so many Francoists. Nowhere was this more evident than in the changes to many women's lives – changes that were in many ways similar to the ones occurring in the Republican zone. Women in the Francoist zone were not recruited to industrial war work; German and Italian aid made this unnecessary. But, just as in the Republican zone, they were mobilized *en masse* to fulfil a series of health and welfare needs generated by the war – in particular operating medical services, orphanages, and emergency food facilities. Women of the urban and provincial middle classes were those who participated most in this mobilization in Francoist Spain.

Many of them joined the women's section of the Falange, the Sección Femenina (SF), an organization that would play an important role in the immediate post-war years when it combined the provision of rudimentary health and social services with surveillance and 'moral' disciplining of Republican families.

15. Women from the relief organization *Auxilio Social*, distributing food in the rebel zone

16. High society women in rebel Spain saluting the flag

Francoists (including Falangists) stressed that they, unlike the 'unnatural' Republicans, were mobilizing women as caregivers and thus in ways that befitted their traditional role. But this political rhetoric could not disguise the fact that the Sección Femenina offered a new public role for significant numbers of women, who saw themselves as engaged in a patriotic enterprise to build a new order in Spain. Not the least of the contradictions that the SF presents is of an 'army' of unmarried, economically independent women officers preaching the gospel of domesticity and subservience to their female clientele. While there are obviously war-related demographic factors that help explain the post-war phenomenon of the SF, it is nonetheless true that over time it played a far from insignificant part in disrupting gender relations and dynamizing social and cultural change.

In both zones the war had a dynamic effect on culture – understood both as a process through which change is mediated and, more narrowly, as specific objects of consumption: songs, films, plays, art work. The Francoists, like the Republicans, created new cultural products specifically designed as propaganda – whether radio programmes (the Francoists' preferred means of disseminating wartime propaganda), or art, or films and newsreels. But so too there was a strong element of continuity. In both Republican and Francoist zones there still existed a thriving mass popular culture, much of which was neither overtly political nor propagandistic. In wartime this became even more socially important precisely because in furnishing a space in which people could dream, it offered a respite from their immediate painful predicament. In both zones this kind of culture included commercialized popular song, cabaret, and café-variety – all of which endured in spite of the moral order campaigns in Franco's territory and (the more ephemeral) disapproval of high-minded revolutionaries in Republican Spain.

Probably the most important of all these popular cultural forms was commercial cinema. The birth of the Republic in 1931 had coincided with the arrival in Spain of sound film, and over the subsequent five years the indigenous film industry grew significantly. For a population of some 24 million there were more than 3,000 picture houses. Hollywood productions in many genres, including romance, musicals, and comedy, were an important component of this popular cinema and remained so during the war in both zones – even though the Francoist authorities generally disapproved of the 'decadence' of such films and subjected them to careful censorship. A great many German and Italian films were also shown in the Francoist zone – although domestic cinematic production, whether of popular or political material, was seriously hampered by the fact that most of the production facilities remained in Republican hands. As a result, both propagandists and commercial producers went to make their films in the studios of Rome and Berlin.

Back in Spain itself, German and Italian technological support of a more decisive nature accelerated at the beginning of 1937, as Hitler and Mussolini decided that a big increase in their military aid was the only way to speed up a rebel victory. The fact that this big push by the dictators came up against Franco's deliberate deceleration of his military advance against the Republic inevitably caused considerable political tension. Fed up with Franco's slowness, Hitler and Mussolini began to wonder about his military competence. They obliged Franco to accept Italians and Germans onto his general staff – something that was scarcely more conducive to his officers than was the presence of Soviet military advisors to professional officers in Republican Spain. Franco, moreover, had to tolerate the existence of Italian military units operating with a degree of autonomy never enjoyed by the International Brigades. This derived from Franco's absolute dependence on Italian military hardware and technology. From January 1937 Italy was also providing Franco with substantial numbers of troops.

The implementation of an efficient system of conscription in the Francoist zone would go some way to addressing this requirement. But even then the need for trained troops meant that the enemy captured on the military front were treated differently to those taken in the dirty war behind Francoist lines. Captured Republican soldiers were in the main recycled – in much the same way as Franco's were by the Republic. Those who had been conscripts to the Republican army were recycled fastest of all, though this did not protect them from political investigation after the war, or from lengthy imprisonment or even a death sentence – which makes it rather more problematic to see the Francoist army as a vehicle of nation-building. Those who had actively volunteered for the Republican army were questioned rigorously before inclusion in Francoist ranks. Republican officers were always subject to harsh interrogation and sometimes executed. Political commissars, if they could be identified as such, received the most brutal treatment of all and were usually shot. All international brigaders, as foreigners and 'mercenaries', fell into the same category and were frequently executed – almost certainly if they were officers or political commissars. In so doing, Franco was breaking the Geneva Conventions on the treatment of prisoners – though later, in 1937, the number of executions decreased because of the need to exchange the internationals for Italian troops captured by the Republicans.

In addition to troops, Franco also increasingly needed airpower that only Germany and Italy could provide. This would give his forces superiority on all except three occasions in the war (the battle for Madrid in late 1936, the battle of Jarama in February 1937, and Guadalajara in March, when the Italians were routed). The price was an ever-increasing dependence on his German and Italian backers. Franco was mortgaging Spain's economic resources increasingly in order to be able to fight his war of annihilation. But unlike the claims frequently made about the Republic's political 'dependence' on the Soviet Union, commentators rarely, if ever, suggest that Francoist Spain was a Nazi or Fascist colony – not even in the immediate post-Civil War period, though the evidence of its status as an 'informal' German colony is substantial (see Chapter 6). But whatever the case, a Francoist victory in the Civil War was necessarily going to mean a Spain that looked favourably on the aggressive territorial expansionism of Italy and Germany. For Franco, in common with the entire Spanish Right, was obsessed with recovering the empire lost in the 19th century, and they saw Nazi Germany's disruption of the international status quo as their best way of achieving this – in the slipstream of fascist victory.

A victory in the Civil War for Franco would at the very least, then, increase the threat to the imperial interests of France and Britain – given Spain's important strategic position at the gateway of communications with their colonies. But though the escalation of German and Italian aid to Franco from spring 1937 onwards caused concern in British circles, it was never enough to bring the policy of Non-Intervention into question. It is often pointed out that British policy-makers had an exaggerated impression of the rate of German rearmament and that this ruled out any possibility of their opposing Hitler over Spain. But this implies a dilemma that never really existed. Even though Britain spent the Civil War vainly trying to detach Italy from Germany, almost no one in the British government felt that a Francoist victory, even if achieved on the back of fascist aid, really posed a threat to British interests.

Most in Britain's governing elites seemed to see their belief in Franco, the 'Christian gentleman', as an antidote to the danger. They were also likely calculating that the requirements of post-war reconstruction – trade and aid – would force Franco into an accommodation with Britain, if for no other reason than his need to raise loans that only the City could provide. If all else failed, then the Royal Navy could blockade Spain. But in all these British extrapolations, there was an unspoken assumption: that the old-world order of politics and finance would remain essentially unaffected by the imperial ambitions of the Third Reich and its bid for continental, even global, conquest. The voices raised against such deadly complacency were isolated and few. Anthony Eden would resign from the cabinet in February 1938, but this had no repercussions on British policy. Very late in the day, at the very end of 1938, Winston Churchill would argue publicly against the appeasement of Germany and Italy through Non-Intervention in Spain. In opposing what was still the dominant view in the Conservative Party, Churchill came close to saying that by pursuing appeasement Britain was letting its class interests overcome its strategic interests.

Franco's fascist allegiances and the creation of a single state party – at least nominally fascist – also risked alienating the entity on which he most closely depended for his political security, the Catholic Church. Both the Spanish Church and the Vatican remained uneasy with the radical aspects of fascism, especially its exaltation of the state, which threatened their own control over the faithful. The Catholic Church also opposed Nazism for its atheistic dimension: hence the Vatican's public condemnation of Hitlerian racism, *Mit brennender Sorge* (*With Burning Sorrow*) issued in mid-March 1937. For Franco, its timing could not have been worse. He was two weeks into the Basque campaign, in which Germany was providing vital air support. He could not risk alienating the Nazi cupola and thus suppressed publication of the Vatican document in the rebel zone. The military authorities also turned a blind eye to the Falange's dissemination of German attacks on it.

But in spite of this, Spain's Catholic hierarchy continued to identify itself unequivocally with Franco. Their shared hostility to rationalism, freemasonry, liberalism, socialism, and communism meant there was far too much ideological common ground for it to have been otherwise. The memory of anticlerical violence in Republican territory had reinforced the ascendancy of ecclesiastical conservatives in the Spanish Church, who were determined to bury the liberal, secular Republic for the challenge it posed to their political power and cultural values. Franco was offering them a chance to do this. While the resulting alliance between Church and dictatorship may superficially have resembled 'throne and altar' variants of earlier times, in fact it constituted something new. For it offered important opportunities for the Church to extend its influence through new disciplinary functions exercised on behalf of the Francoist state. Nor was this simply about the predictable areas of educational control and censorship; Church personnel would also play a key role in the running of prisons, reformatories, and other correctional facilities.

In contrast to Spain's Catholic Church, the Vatican had to proceed rather more cautiously. Its sympathies lay with the Francoist cause, but it also had to consider the fate of Catholics in Republican Spain. Even more important in Vatican calculations was the potential damage to the credibility of Catholicism itself, if its strength in Spain came to be perceived as the result of Francoist military conquest. 'You may conquer but you will never convince': the Vatican's dilemma is encapsulated in these words of the Catholic philosopher Miguel de Unamuno, who uttered them in October 1936 in defiance of the rebels' exultant battle cry 'Long live death!' – just two months before he died under house arrest in Salamanca, the capital of rebel Spain. The dilemma was evident too in the Vatican's complex diplomacy during the war. Relations with the Republic were not formally broken – indeed, they were even reactivated in the latter part of the war (see Chapter 5). The Vatican also made unsuccessful attempts in 1937 to broker a peace settlement with Franco on behalf of the Basques. Most tellingly, it was only in the spring of 1938, when a rebel victory seemed imminent, that the Vatican would establish full diplomatic relations with Franco's Spain.

Franco and his advisors worked hard to integrate the traditional components of his power base with the modern ones. This was evident on ceremonial occasions in the mixing of fascist symbols with those from Spain's imperial and authoritarian Catholic past. Many argue that the important role played by the Catholic Church indicates that Francoism can best be defined as an old-fashioned dictatorship. It abolished mass democracy, and it did so without recourse to any novel or modern means. Certainly the self-proclaimed fascist Falange always remained a subordinate (if important) element in the regime. But there are other ways of approaching the question of what Francoism was.

All of the political forces that made up Francoism explicitly rejected parliamentary democracy and the rule of constitutional law as vile symptoms of the liberal age. But, unlike traditional conservatives, Francoists did not view these things as external political forms that could simply be banned. Rather, they were seen as having already been incorporated into a large part of the Spanish population, as having, in short, 'infected' it. The issue was no longer the body politic, but the biological body of the 'nation' and the total control thereof. This was what Franco's military strategy was about: the internal colonization of the metropolis, in order to destroy the 'alien' Republican nation/culture therein. The Franco regime constructed its political practices and goals in the light of this key belief, the need for 'purification' – something which, by definition, meant it had to go much further than old-fashioned authoritarianism in order to remedy the 'problem'.

Where we see Francoism most clearly 'going further' is in what it did to the defeated. There is a startling uniformity about the degradation and objectification inflicted upon hundreds of thousands of Republican prisoners after the end of the military conflict (discussed further in Chapter 6). Of particular significance was the remarkable need of their captors to break not only Republicans' bodies but also their minds before killing them, and even when they were not killed, to leave them, as it were, psychologically 'reconfigured' by their experience of prison, labour camp, youth reformatory, and myriad other forms of judicial, civic, and economic repression. This huge process of manufacturing an anti-nation, an 'anti-Spain' or excluded other – which for more than a decade after the end of military hostilities consumed vast amounts of the country's energy and resources – was, paradoxically, a crucial part of the regime's construction (or 'reconstruction' as many Francoists saw it) of a homogenous and hierarchized Spain.

Also integral to the building of this nation was the Civil War itself. Mobilization had to a certain extent made a reality of the ideal 'Spain' projected in Francoist propaganda: a monolithic national community primed for self-sacrifice. The suffering and loss endured by conservative sectors of Spanish society during the war helped forge a Francoist identity just as surely as other forms of suffering and loss created a Republican identity in the opposing zone. But what was specific about Francoism was the way that this experience of loss was brutally coopted by the regime for specific political ends – first and foremost, its own legitimation. Crucial to this would be the all-embracing machinery of denunciation implemented by Franco after his military victory on 1 April 1939. Spaniards were exhorted to denounce their neighbours to military and civilian tribunals. This vast process, discussed in Chapter 6, made millions of 'ordinary Spaniards' complicit in the repression.

In February 1939 Franco secretly agreed to join Germany, Japan, and Italy in the Anti-Comintern pact. He signed the following month and publicly declared Spain's membership of the pact immediately after he achieved victory in the Civil War. In Franco's clear political alignment with the fascist powers, ideology as well as strategic interest played a part. Certainly, Franco's enthusiasm for the Nazi new order in Europe was about more than the search for new Spanish colonies.

Ideological rapprochement between Francoism and Nazism was nevertheless problematized by the question of Catholicism. Nazism was new precisely because those at its radical leading edge sought to take a 'purified' German (and European) society beyond allegiances to Churches – Catholic or otherwise – indeed, to take society beyond the foundational ethics of Judaeo-Christian religion itself. But the Catholic Church was Francoism's closest ally in the work of 'purification', in the disciplining of bodies and minds. No group – not even the Falange's most pro-Nazi sector – ever dreamed of leaving religion behind.

But nor should this observation lead us to suppose that the Franco dictatorship was simply a traditional form of authoritarianism. Francoism took radical measures against wealthy property-owning sectors who had adopted a more or less liberal political position in the 1930s. It passed legislation that permitted a massive forced transfer of wealth and property to the Francoist state – that is, when this had not already occurred in a *de facto* way, by right of 'conquest'. The order built after 1939 by Church and state was a new one – notwithstanding the presence within it of members of the pre-war elites. It was also as savagely hierarchizing and discriminatory as Nazism's, for all that the Spanish model was not racially based. The whole enterprise of Francoism sprang from a 'modern' need: the brutal management of conflictive social change. The regime was modern too in its cooption *en masse* of Spaniards through the mechanism of denunciation. Finally also, Francoism would be modern because in the end so much about the processes of social and economic change that had conjured it would escape the regime's capacity for management – brutal or otherwise.

Chapter 5
The Republic besieged

A society struggling to progress is reduced by external aggression to
levels of hardship and sheer survival that the aggressor then adduces
as proof of the impossibility of social progress.

(Eduardo Galeano)

To fight on because there was no other choice, even if winning was
not possible, then to salvage what we could – and at the very least
our self respect . . . . Why go on resisting? Quite simply because we
knew what capitulation would mean.

(Juan Negrín)

By the middle of 1937, the Republic faced an increasingly
well-equipped enemy regularly and efficiently supplied with the
best-quality military hardware direct from German and Italian
factories. Non-Intervention did nothing to stop or even slow up
this flow of war materiel. Often it was sent in ships chartered
and paid for by Nazi Germany but which sailed under flags of
convenience and were thus beyond the reach of Non-Intervention
Committee controls. Given its relative proximity to Spain, Italy used
its own merchant fleet, protected by the Italian air force or by its
own warships, which no one, certainly not the Royal Navy, was
prepared to challenge. This assured Franco of a rapid and virtually
uninterrupted supply – the timeliness of deliveries often being a
much more important factor than their scale. German and Italian

supplies were also unloaded in Portuguese ports with the complicity of the authorities. Since the aid from Germany and Italy came direct from government, it also arrived with fully integrated technical support and logistical back-up. Up against this, Soviet-procured aid to the Republic could not compensate quantitatively or qualitatively. It could thus only ever offer the Republic scant survival.

Stalin was neither willing nor able to send precious material from Soviet factories in a quantity that could have allowed the Spanish Republic to compete on equal terms on the battlefield once Italy and German stepped up their support for Franco at the end of 1936. In 1937 Soviet industrial production was still in a turmoil of reorganization, made worse by the purges, and throughout the war in Spain real Soviet production levels remained anything up to 50% below the published ones. Given this situation, it is surprising that Stalin sent even as much domestically produced materiel to the Republic as he did. This was high quality – most crucially the planes and tanks – and, as we have seen, it was vital to Republican survival, especially at the start. But much of the 'Soviet aid' that kept the Republic ticking over did not originate in Soviet factories at all, rather it was obtained from elsewhere by the Soviet Union acting as a broker.

The Republic needed the Soviet Union's services because Non-Intervention stopped it from purchasing war materiel on its own behalf on the open market – even though this embargo, which prevented a democratically elected government from buying arms to defend itself, probably contravened international law. As an extension of the partisan logic of Non-Intervention, nor were there, so the Republican government discovered, any safe channels in the Western banking sector through which it could mobilize its financial resources for war. Republican gold and silver deposited in one French bank would be frozen by the authorities, and a major bank in Britain obstructed funds that were to be used for Republican arms purchases – although the British banking sector placed no similar constraints on Franco's agents. These were the reasons that had underlain the decision of the outgoing Republican cabinet, in consultation with Bank of Spain officials at the end of August 1936, to transfer Spain's gold reserves out of the country – so they could be mobilized without impediment to finance the war effort. (This cabinet, it should also be noted, was composed entirely of ministers from Spain's republican parties – neither the Socialist Party nor the Spanish Communist Party was yet part of the wartime government.) The first consignments of gold left beleaguered Madrid in mid-September, destined for the southeastern port of Cartagena. Once it became clear that the Soviet Union was prepared to offer military assistance, the Republican authorities agreed in October 1936 to transfer the gold there. Mexico was the only other country prepared to assist Republican Spain as a broker. But while it provided valuable and relatively disinterested assistance, especially at the start of the war, the Soviet Union had much greater resources and leverage internationally than did Mexico and was thus much more useful to the Republic.

Apart from the materiel that came direct from the Soviet Union, most of the armaments procured by the Republic through intermediaries came from Eastern Europe and, in practice, mainly from Poland. At first sight this is surprising, since not only was the military dictatorship there a signatory to the Non-Intervention agreement, it was also politically sympathetic to Franco. But selling to the Republic was too lucrative an opportunity to forgo – all the more especially as this allowed Poland to offload obsolete and defective stock, thereby raising revenue for its own crisis-ridden treasury and re-armament programme.

Non-Intervention meant that the Republic always paid massively over the odds for the materiel it secured. The captive status of the buyer and an insufficient supply led to graft, corruption, and hugely inflated prices – creating what was effectively a black market in arms that the Republic, and only the Republic, was forced to use in order to stay alive. It was also hard for the Republicans to find people capable of navigating the murky world of international arms trafficking – the wheeler-dealers tended to be in Franco's camp. Republican procurement agents were often fleeced by middle men and assorted opportunists (not infrequently state officials) who were only too keen to get their hands on Republican gold. For, unlike German and Italian aid to Franco, which came entirely on credit, the Republic had to pay cash up front. This was the case whether it was purchasing from arms dealers, other intermediaries, or from the Soviet Union – which also extracted maximum revenue from the Republic.

The fact that the Republic was forced to sweep up a motley array of sources in order to arm itself led to situations that would have been comic, had it not been for the desperate nature of the circumstances: guns arrived with incompatible ammunition or with instructions in obscure foreign languages, or materiel came without technical or logistical back-up or turned out to be antique weaponry more appropriate to a museum than the front line.

But the Republic's armaments problems did not end with supply; delivery was also a nightmare. The Soviet Union was far from Spain. The Republic lacked merchant ships and the Soviet Union was a land-based power that could not make good that lack. It was, in any case, reluctant to risk its small merchant marine in the lengthy and hazardous journey to Spain, and after the sinking of the Soviet vessel Komsomol in December 1936, it required the Republic to provide transport for all the war materiel it either sent or procured. But the Republic, with crippling arms prices to pay and an ever-growing population to feed, as refugees flooded in from the other zone, did not have the resources to charter vessels on an adequate scale – as the Germans did for Franco.

From the start, the Germans and Italians had attacked shipping bound for Republican ports, even though they had no authority to do so. Even worse, from the late summer of 1937 their backing allowed Franco to blockade the ports on Spain's Mediterranean coast – thus cutting the Republic off from any direct supply of arms. From this point all military aid to the Republic had to come across the land frontier from France. In theory this should have been the end for the Republic, since France was a signatory to Non-Intervention. But fears of fascist encirclement led the French government to pursue a more ambiguous policy of 'relaxed Non-Intervention'. This meant that the border between France and Spain was permeable – but unpredictably so. Aid came across, but it could also be blocked completely or held up for lengthy periods. 'Relaxed Non-Intervention' made it possible for the Republic to survive after the Mediterranean had been blockaded, but it made it impossible for it to sustain offensives because it could never guarantee the quality or consistency of its military supply. All in all, this was no way to have to fight a war. It took its toll on the battlefield capabilities of the Republican army – including by the increased psychological stress it inflicted – especially on those in command, who were haunted by a constant knowledge of their lack of reserves.

In a bid to take the pressure off the remainder of the Republican north after the fall of the Basque Country in June 1937, the Republicans launched a diversionary summer offensive on the previously inactive Aragon front in northeast Spain. With the advantage of surprise, they made rapid progress, added to which the Republican army was by the middle of 1937 a competent fighting force. It had talented officers – if too few of them – and was led by Colonel (later General) Vicente Rojo, the Republican chief of staff who, unlike Franco, was an imaginative and innovative strategist. Rojo, a professional officer from before the war, was personally conservative and a practising Catholic, but his commitment to the Republic was firm and unambiguous, galvanized by his experience of Madrid's resistance. The key to the choice Rojo made – for the Republic and against Franco – probably lies in the fact that he had not pursued a career in the Army of Africa and was aloof from its ethos. His reputation, from his time as a teacher in the

Military Academy, was as that rarest of creatures in Spanish military culture – a technical modernizer and innovator.

The construction of the new Republican army itself involved both innovation and improvisation. While its Spanish commanders and officers had important assistance from Soviet technical advisors, these were a scarce resource – between 600 and 800 people at any one time across the whole of the Republican zone (some 3,000 Soviet personnel serving in Spain during the whole war). And for all the valuable qualitative assistance of these military engineers, technicians, strategists, and experts in irregular warfare, this should not prevent us from recognizing the scale of the Spanish Republicans' own achievement in constructing a new fighting force. Inevitably, the circumstances in which this new force was born and the necessary rapidity of its construction meant it had structural defects – most notably a lack of middle-ranking officers (the group that most heavily supported Franco) and insufficient internal articulation within and between its regional groupings. As Rojo himself commented, 'we have five armies, but not one'. Repeated defeats in the second half of 1937 would also further erode its best-trained cadres and intensify the internal disarticulation.

Nevertheless, it was an army whose morale remained remarkably high throughout the war in spite of the defeats. In contrast to the spread of war weariness and demoralization on the Republican home front by 1938, morale in the army remained relatively intact, and while desertion occurred, it remained a comparatively limited phenomenon. Partly this had to do with the intense experience of front-line comradeship and solidarity, and also with the (related) role of the political commissars (discussed in Chapter 3). In part it doubtless also reflected the priority the Republican government placed on supplying and provisioning troops over the civilian population. Compared to other wars of the modern age, we know relatively little about the values and sentiments of ordinary recruits in the Republican army, but there is no reason to doubt the strength of the wartime socialization process that occurred through the experience of combat and mobilization – a process that happened to some extent on the home front too, problems of morale notwithstanding. It inculcated a strong sense of Republican identity in many who had previously been indifferent. This we can gauge from the fact that people with no history of pre-war political militancy were among the hundreds of thousands who took the road into exile in 1939.

But the Republicans' courage and resourcefulness on the Aragon front were not enough to give them the upper hand for long. As desperate battles raged at Quinto and Belchite, armaments destined for the Republic sat at French border controls, blocked by the vagaries of 'relaxed' Non-Intervention. Nor did the Republic have enough adequately trained reserve troops. And if Non-Intervention made it difficult to equip adequately the Republican army, it made it impossible to equip its reserves. By late summer 1937, it was clear that the Republican offensive was unsustainable, and could not prevent Franco's conquest of the north. The fall of Asturias (Avilés and Gijón) came in October 1937 and meant the loss of the coal industry and the Republic's northern armies – some 200,000 soldiers. In both respects it was a blood loss that ended the possibility of the Republic achieving an outright military victory in the Civil War. What happened at Teruel in the bitter winter of 1937–8 made evident that impossibility.

The battle of Teruel, capital of the bleakest of Aragon's provinces, was another of Rojo's diversionary campaigns. The objective was to deflect Franco's renewed focus on Madrid. The *Generalísimo* ignored his advisors – German, Italian, and Spanish – and diverted troops to Teruel. He was anxious not to lose a square inch of territory, but even more to take advantage of an opportunity to annihilate large numbers of the enemy – including some of the Republican army's best units. For unlike the Republicans, Franco did not have to worry about using up reserves, as these could be readily and easily replaced.

The battle was fought in the depths of the winter of 1937–8, one of the bitterest Spain has ever seen. Blizzard conditions prevented Franco from using mechanized transport and planes. Soldiers died from exposure, others had to have frost-bitten limbs amputated. The Republicans captured the city in early January 1938, but they were unable to resist Franco's counter-offensive. Teruel was the turning point of the war in that it confirmed once and for all that the sheer materiel superiority of Franco's forces could not be countered by Republican courage or tactical cunning. General Rojo had a strategic genius that Franco lacked, but, unlike Franco, Rojo was unable every time to implement his strategy. In the last analysis, Republican vulnerability was inscribed in the fact that all Rojo's offensives were reactive strategies and diversions. At Teruel, after another costly defence of a small advance, the Republicans had to retreat.

By late February, the city had been retaken by Franco's forces, who also captured nearly 15,000 prisoners and vast quantities of military equipment. By 1938, the Republic's cumulative losses of trained soldiers – after the collapse of the northern front and now at Teruel – were forcing it to call up ever younger and older drafts. The Republic's need here was now much greater than Franco's. But raw recruits were a poor replacement for the seasoned troops it had lost. This constant erosion also took its toll, a further factor inhibiting the performance of the Republican army.

The outcome at Teruel also required an adjustment in the thinking of Republican prime minister Juan Negrín. Since taking over the government in May 1937, he had pursued a two-pronged strategy of military resistance and international diplomacy designed to get Non-Intervention lifted or, at the very least, to secure belligerent rights for the Republic. The May cabinet changes were crucially about this: the breakthrough to power of political leaders (backed by the Republican president) who understood that the outcome of the Spanish war would ultimately be decided in the chancelleries of Europe. So it was imperative that the Republic win support there through much more proactive diplomacy. In these terms, Juan Negrín was 'the necessary leader'. Born in 1892, the same year as Franco, into one of the wealthiest families in Las Palmas de Gran Canaria, Negrín was educated extensively abroad. He qualified as a doctor in Germany, where he also pursued medical research. Aged only 30, he was appointed to the chair of physiology at Madrid University. He supported the Republic over Spain's monarchical establishment because he was a constitutional liberal, and, like many others of his generation, joined the Spanish Socialist Party because he saw it as the best instrument for modernizing Spain and opening it up to Europe. Negrín was formidably intelligent – politically as well as academically – and an immensely astute observer of European and world politics. Urbane, cosmopolitan, and multi-lingual, he had excellent contacts abroad and so, unlike his prime-ministerial predecessor, he could function fluently in the world of international diplomacy.

Initially Negrín's diplomatic efforts to secure belligerent rights for the Republic were focused on France, whose sense of vulnerability had been increased by British overtures to Italy. Such rights would not have solved the underlying problem, since Britain would continue to do its utmost to block arms sales to the Republic. But the granting of belligerent rights would at least have allowed the Republic to purchase arms openly and also properly to defend its war materiel en route to Spain – for it could muster sufficient warships to serve as escorts in Mediterranean waters. Not least it would also have allowed the Republic to search 'neutral' (and especially Italian) shipping and thus to impede arms shipments to Franco. What happened at Teruel did not outwardly change Negrín's strategy. But it did begin to reconfigure it internally. The loss of the industrial north combined with Franco's blockade of the Republic's Mediterranean ports, and the steady attrition of its army obliged Negrín to look for a means of bringing Franco to the negotiating table. Negrín also understood, however, that there was not the least chance of achieving this unless the Republic's military resistance remained determined and effective.

But the Republic's military situation was about to become critical. After recapturing Teruel, Franco's troops were poised to sweep through Aragon. There was little the Republicans could do to stop them – even though France, fearful of the consequences of Hitler's occupation of Austria (*Anschluss*) on 12 March 1938, opened up its frontier to allow arms to pass unhindered. But by now it was too late. Franco had a 20% advantage in terms of men and an overwhelming one in terms of aircraft, artillery, and other equipment. Abandoning his habitual caution, in mid-March Franco launched against a Republican army not yet recovered from its battering at Teruel the *Blitzkrieg* so often advocated by his German and Italian advisors. Barcelona was terror bombed by Italian planes in an attempt to break civilian morale. Under a curtain of fire provided by 1,000 Italian and German aircraft, plus armoured cars and tanks (including captured Russian ones), over 100,000 troops spearheaded by elite Moroccan and Italian forces surged across the River Ebro.

In the first days of April 1938, the northern wing of their advance into Aragon took the city of Lerida and then the important power station at Tremp, temporarily blacking out Barcelona and reducing its industrial output thereafter. Meanwhile, the Francoists' central units drove down the Ebro valley to the Castellón-Valencian coast. On 15 April they took the small coastal town of Vinaroz, reached the Mediterranean, and split Republican Spain into two: Catalonia and the centre-south zone (see Figure 17).

The next day Britain signed the Anglo-Italian agreement and continued to pressure France to close the frontier – even though Britain's own merchant ships were still being sunk by Italy. The ruptured Republic faced a massive crisis on both its military and home fronts.

Militarily, the war might even have been over at this point. In the period immediately after the Republic was split into two, its defences were more vulnerable than they would ever be at any

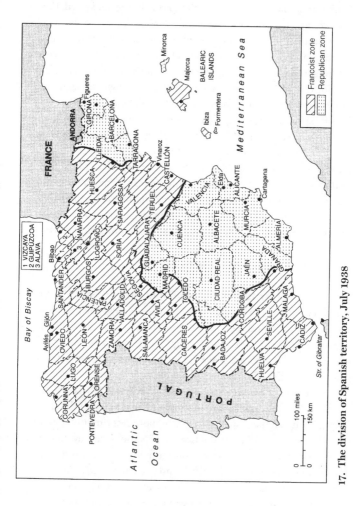

17. The division of Spanish territory, July 1938

subsequent point in the war. Its army was in disarray and the front was broken between Vinaroz and Barcelona. If Franco had gone straight on for Barcelona, then he could not have been stopped. With Catalonia in his power and the French frontier sealed, the war would have been over more quickly. But Franco, to the astonishment of the Republic's political leaders, its military high command, and not a few of his own high-ranking officers, diverted troops south instead for a major attack on Valencia. Partly he did this for fear that a head-on assault on Catalonia would frighten France into intervening there militarily in defence of the Republic. In retrospect, it is unlikely that this would have occurred, but after the French reaction to the *Anschluss*, Franco was not prepared to risk provoking its government any further. More importantly, however, to have launched an offensive against Catalonia at that point would have left a substantial Republican force in the centre-south zone. Turning away from Catalonia in spring 1938 and towards the centre-south army, thus lengthening the conflict, was about maximizing the destruction and demoralization visited on the Republic's human resources. It was, then, entirely consistent with Franco's underlying war aims.

The survival of the Republic beyond April 1938 depended on the rapid reorganization of its armies and the political galvanization of its home front. Continued military resistance was seen by Negrín as a crucial means of increasing the diplomatic pressure on Britain and France. They feared that the longer the Spanish conflict went on, the more likely it was to explode into a general European conflagration that would draw them in inexorably. These fears, combined with the British government's distaste for all things Republican, led them successfully to oppose Negrín's bid to have Non-Intervention lifted at the League of Nations in May. In public Negrín declared his continuing commitment to all-out resistance. But, in the hope of turning British and French anxieties to the Republic's advantage, throughout the second half of 1938, Negrín engaged in an intense round of personal diplomacy to try to persuade the great powers to broker international mediation as a way of ending the conflict in Spain. But this would be much harder to achieve now because the division of the Republican zone indicated its weakness not its strength, and Franco would scarcely be inclined to negotiate over what he believed he could take by force.

Maintaining Republican resistance was also dependent on access to an external supply of armaments – however tenuous. But the situation at the French frontier was now precarious in the extreme. In mid-June the border, opened in the wake of *Anschluss*, was once again closed. The new French government, of more conservative hue, was less inclined to tolerate a permeable frontier. 'Relaxed Non-Intervention' was over. The government also froze Republican financial assets in French banks. This was the price exacted by Franco before he would agree exports to France of the pyrites crucial to its rearmament programme and in which the north of Spain was uniquely rich in Europe.

By mid-1938, the Republic's gold reserves were perilously close to being exhausted. Negrín had always been clear that the war would be over the day its last gold-peseta was spent. Certainly, he was right that the Republic could not access major sources of credit as Franco could. But the Republic was able to eke out its defence beyond the summer of 1938 courtesy of $60 million credit provided by the Soviet Union. Since the outbreak of the Sino-Japanese war in early July, Spain had in fact been displaced in Soviet foreign policy considerations. Soviet technical advisors were recalled during the summer. Stalin also agreed to the withdrawal of the International Brigades. Mainly staffed by Spaniards anyway by 1938, the presence of foreign volunteers in Republican Spain was now of little more than symbolic importance. Stalin no longer believed the Republic could win in the face of Francoist blockade and British obduracy – something that had also rendered impossible his own preference for an agreement of collective security with Britain and France against an expansionist Nazi Germany. Nevertheless, the longer the Republic went on resisting, the longer it absorbed German energies, and the better that was for Soviet defences. So, although whatever the Republic used of the credit would almost certainly be irrecuperable, it was still considered money well spent.

Given that Soviet support was vital to the Republic's continued ability to resist, Negrín needed to keep totally secret his search for international mediation. This partly explains his insistence on taking personal charge of diplomacy. Negrín made a number of trips abroad in 1938 – always ostensibly for other purposes but during which he had discreet, informal exchanges with Francoist representatives, and on occasion with those of Nazi Germany too. Even his own government ministers were excluded from this intelligence loop – which over time would lead to misunderstandings and mounting discontent. But Negrín was adamant about secrecy because he realized that knowledge of his strategic diplomatic objectives would erode the will of the Republican army to fight and of civilians to endure hunger and privation. Negrín himself was absolutely clear about the value of a strategic resistance aimed at imposing peace conditions on Franco. Chief among these in Negrín's mind was a guarantee of no reprisals against the defeated. He also wanted assurances over the constitutional and territorial integrity of Spain which Negrín feared would be endangered by the political and economic ambitions of Italy and Germany, to whom Franco would end the war massively in debt.

Negrín fervently believed that the Republic's capacity to resist depended crucially on the psychological state of its soldiers and civilians. Everything, then, had to be geared to improving or at least maintaining Republican morale. On the military front this saw the guerrilla corps of the Republican army involved in an innovative commando operation in May 1938. They successfully liberated several hundred Republican soldiers captured during the fall of the northern front in autumn 1937 from their fortress-gaol on the south coast at Carchuna (Motril) – just across from the Republican lines. This action not only boosted morale in the grim days after the great retreats through Aragon, it also provided a much-needed source of trained soldiers after the cumulative losses of the previous autumn and winter. Participating too in the Carchuna 'jailbreak' were two American international brigaders, Irv Goff and Bill Aalto, who had fought in the guerrilla since early 1937.

Negrín's belief in the crucial importance of morale had also underlain his decision at the beginning of April 1938 to remove as war minister his great friend and political intimate Indalecio Prieto, the most important politician of the pre-war Republic. Intelligent and energetic, Prieto was also notorious for his public pessimism over the war. But he overstepped the mark when, at the very moment that Negrín was doing his utmost to ensure the French frontier remained open in the aftermath of Teruel, Prieto announced to the French ambassador that the Republic was finished. The difference between Negrín and Prieto was not their intellectual grasp of the Republic's position, but rather their subjective response to it. Negrín drew strength from adversity, while Prieto seemed to cave in before the bleakness. Negrín honed down his energies to a single fierce point and focused only on the matter in hand – how to maintain an army in the field, supplied and fed. But in 'sacking' Prieto, Negrín exposed the growing divisions within the Republican political class.

Political divisions inside the Republican camp increased across 1938 in direct proportion to the military and diplomatic defeats it sustained. Inevitably the huge and growing external pressures – chronic shortage imposed by Non-Intervention and the blockade of Republican ports and an international diplomatic horizon growing bleaker every day – began to exacerbate internal political differences, many of which pre-dated the war.

One of the most subtly erosive was the enmity between the central Republican government and the regional government of Catalonia, the *Generalitat*. A major consequence of the Barcelona May Days of 1937 had been that the centre moved to increase its powers. The

Generalitat lost control of public order in Catalonia – which had been the jewel in the crown of its autonomy statute, granted by the Republic in 1932. Then, in October 1937, Negrín moved the central Republican government to Barcelona and assumed direct control of the Catalan war industry – a crucial source of materiel after the fall of the industrial north (where centre-periphery tensions had also contributed to the collapse). Morale in Catalonia was badly affected, for it was the region with by far the deepest independent political and cultural traditions in all Spain. But for the central Republican government – composed of highly centralist-minded republicans, socialists, and communists – the lesson of the May Days was that nothing must ever again be allowed to threaten war production or military resistance.

Relations between the two governments became increasingly mired in resource-sapping jurisdictional disputes. The sources of friction were numerous – ranging from the comparatively minor, if bitter, competition over which of the two could occupy the most prestigious city buildings as government offices, through complaints over the importation of 'foreign' (Castilian) factory managers and police to serve in Catalonia. There was also a serious clash in the summer of 1938 over Negrín's determination to militarize justice. This saw a further centralization of power and ultimately played its part in the departure of the Catalan (and Basque) representatives from Negrín's cabinet in August 1938.

There is no doubt that during the war Negrín showed himself unsympathetic to political Catalanism because he saw it as engaging in petty provincial squabbles while Rome, or rather Spain, burned. Negrín's inclinations, in the classic centralist tradition of progressive republicanism, probably also made him hostile to Catalanism *per se*. Some of his pronouncements were needlessly inflammatory. But the main accusation levelled by Catalan nationalists, that Negrín's liberal constitutionalism was a sham, simply does not stand up to scrutiny.

From the time Negrín entered politics he had sought measures that would strengthen Spain's constitutional order. (For this reason too he had been almost alone in 1932 in arguing that the death penalty should be implemented against General Sanjurjo, the titular head of the first military rebellion against Republican democracy.) Because of their anti-constitutionality, Negrín abhorred the popular revolutionary committees that abounded in the Republican zone in 1936, nor was he sympathetic to their collectivist credo. He stood for a liberal market-based economy and many of his wartime measures (Negrín had begun as treasury minister in September 1936) were designed to reinforce this model over collectivist and anti-capitalist ones. Unlike Franco, who would punish Spaniards for their beliefs and thus for acts of omission (that is, not actively supporting the military rebellion), Negrín as prime minister put in place judicial mechanisms to restore expropriated property to all Spanish citizens irrespective of their politics, provided they had not been actively involved in the military coup. Negrín also oversaw the implementation of measures – for example, in the prison service – designed to professionalize (and thus depoliticize) hiring policy. Negrín's declaration of Republican war aims, the 13 points, published in May 1938 as a basis for brokering a peace, were a model of liberal constitutionality.

Included prominently in the 13 points was an affirmation of liberty of conscience. Nor was this merely a statement of good intentions designed for external consumption. For Negrín the normalization of the Catholic Church's position was a litmus test of Republican constitutionality. Negrín was himself a secular rationalist, but he was not anticlerical – indeed, his own brother had taken holy orders. By the summer of 1937, private Catholic worship was already permitted, but progress towards the reopening of churches was necessarily slower. Negrín certainly did not lack the will – as Catalan Christian democrats have testified. But the Spanish Church hierarchy's public backing for Franco's coup had created a dense and fraught atmosphere in the Republican zone that could not be conjured overnight. The prime minister proceeded with caution and discretion, by mid-1938 his efforts were beginning to bear fruit and in October, with the tacit support of the Vatican, Negrín appointed a specific entity to oversee the reintroduction of public worship. This was planned first for Catalonia, and was well on the way to being realized when the military collapse of the region supervened in early 1939.

The second great tension in the wartime political life of the Republic was the growing rift between Spanish socialists and communists – the two mass movements sustaining the war effort. This conflict had its roots in longstanding organizational and personal rivalries that were massively intensified by the war. By 1938 the rivalry was becoming fatally entangled with disputes at the socialist party cupola and with the estrangement of a number of party leaders from Negrín, especially after Prieto's departure from the cabinet. Ultimately, this wartime conflict was driven to a great extent by the mounting demoralization and desperation of many leading socialists faced with the plight of the isolated Republic. Even though they had no alternative to propose, they criticized Negrín's resistance strategy as increasingly irresponsible. In part, this was because they were unaware of its crucial concomitant – his intense, but of course secret, diplomacy. But also they were resentful because Negrín was coming to rely more and more on Spanish communist personnel over and above members of his own party.

What appealed to Negrín was not communist ideology (indeed, many post-18 July 1936 communists were rather light on this, if strong on their party-movement as a community of the select). Nor was he unaware that the party's agenda differed in important respects from his own. But what Negrín needed in the 'here and now' was the communists' unfailing discipline and, above all, their unquestioning commitment to a policy of resistance. Their discipline thus became his instrument.

Party discipline certainly also reflected the policy of the Comintern, though the Spanish communist leaders were not merely its mouthpiece. In a fast-moving war, they had had to become a real leadership capable of responding to the huge number of war-related tasks demanded of the party. Nor were the Spanish communist leaders always in agreement with the Comintern. In the summer of 1937, when it proposed that the party should campaign for new elections to the Republican parliament, the Spanish leaders concurred with the rest of the Republic's political forces that this would be highly counter-productive. The proposal went no further. In 1938 Spanish party leaders also successfully resisted Comintern suggestions that the communist ministerial representation in Negrín's cabinet should cease – as a way of trying to break the international diplomatic log jam. In the end the Spanish Communist Party would pay a high price for its association with all-out military resistance. As war weariness mounted and people began to lose hope in the face of the diplomatic impasse, even many of those who had themselves joined communist organizations in 1936 would turn to discharge their frustration and despair on the party.

Hunger too eroded hope. By spring 1938, the Republic was manifestly unable to deliver the basic requirements of daily life to its civilian population – swollen by constant waves of refugees arriving from rebel-conquered territory; 25,000 more refugees came with the collapse of Aragon in spring 1938, which meant that by the end of the war there would be around 600,000 refugees in Republican Spain, including 200,000 children. The big grain-producing regions lay in Francoist territory and the Republic had never been able to import sufficient food to meet the shortfall – lacking funds as it did because of the exhorbitant armaments prices it was required to pay courtesy of Non-Intervention. Now things were worse. Franco's blockade of the Mediterranean coast meant that the Republic's centre-south zone had no direct access to supplies.

Catalonia also needed food urgently. But communication between the two Republican zones was extremely hazardous (even radio

18. Child street-seller in Republican Spain

contact was uncertain and intermittent). German and Italian submarines torpedoed sea traffic, putting Barcelona out of reach of Valencia, except by aircraft. These had a more limited capacity, however, and were also subject to enemy attack. Food for Catalonia had to come from France. But the increasingly fraught politics of the border made it a precarious source and, anyway, the amount of food crossing over came nowhere near meeting the need. Catalonia, with its massive number of refugees, suffered acute shortages.

All over Republican territory deprivation and deteriorating material conditions produced an acute sensation of vulnerability, isolation, and danger. The Republic's political legitimacy was eroded as defeat followed defeat, and the subsistence crisis escalated. Shortage, inflation, population dislocation, threatening starvation, and epidemic disease all made it impossible for the Republic credibly to project – in terms of welfare reform and other social benefits – the 'state side' of a social contract with those who were fighting and dying for it. The Republic could no longer embody a vision of a positive, progressive future. Under such intense pressure, with morale under siege along with everything else, the Republican zone inevitably became increasingly militarized – even though this undermined its own democratic *raison d'être*. The war – and more specifically the desperate bid to keep resistance alive – was consuming everything.

Desperately short of troops by 1938, the Republican authorities had little choice but to step up conscription and to use increasingly aggressive and intrusive methods to achieve it. This was one of the main functions of the Republican military intelligence service. Its personnel attempted to encourage denunciations of draft dodgers, while family members caught aiding and abetting them could be severely punished under Republican law. This created resentment and fear inside often quite small communities, and the effects were hugely erosive. Those on the receiving end inevitably came to feel hostile towards the besieged Republic. In rural areas too, social tensions increased as a result of soldiers living off the land. Republican army policy forbade unofficial 'requisition', but it still occurred, and especially at times of maximum stress and dislocation. For example, in the great retreats through Aragon following the division of Republican territory in April 1938, numerous acts of violence were committed against civilians – including Republican officials, such as the policeman who was killed when he tried to stop retreating soldiers stealing bread from a village bakery.

An increasingly demoralized population also provided fertile ground for the fifth column, whose confidence and activity levels had been boosted by the successive territorial advances of Franco's forces and knowledge of the stranglehold in which diplomatic isolation held the Republic. Quite aside from the activities of isolated pro-Franco individuals who spread rumour and misinformation, all major Republican cities had within them by late 1937 organized networks of spies and saboteurs which posed a far more serious threat. Republican military intelligence successfully dismantled a number of them. However, dealing with the 'enemy within' involved surveillance and interrogation techniques that violated the Republican commitment to constitutional guarantees and the equality of all citizens before the law.

This conflict between the imperatives of war and the obligation to preserve the civil liberties for which one fights is something with which far longer-established and more favourably placed democratic polities than Republican Spain still struggle, and fall short. It was a dilemma that Franco of course never faced: both during and after the war, he reduced the judicial process to a branch of state terror. The wartime Republic, in contrast, behaved like a democracy at war. Constitutional rights were curtailed when Negrín introduced special courts to try cases of espionage and treason, but the Republic nevertheless maintained a constitutional framework – no mean feat in itself given the newness of Republican democracy and its besieged condition. The judiciary investigated abuses committed by the police and the prison service – which included cruel treatment of detainees/inmates and unlawful killings. The very fact that these actions were defined as abuses tells us a great deal. In the Francoist zone, which was never under siege, dehumanization, torture, and unlawful killing of the enemy were seen not as abuses but as a prophylactic administered by power.

Not even when the Republic was fighting for its life, in the last, gargantuan battle at the Ebro between July and November 1938, did the immense pressures of the war override constitutional guarantees. In October 1938, the POUM leaders were brought to trial and convicted of having publicly supported an illegal rebellion (that of May 1937 in Barcelona) against the Republican state at war. That they were brought before the courts at this late stage was certainly about making an example of them in order to discipline the home front at a time when its disintegration threatened. But the POUM's was not a show trial. In spite of the Spanish Communist Party leadership's best efforts to influence proceedings, and thus to cashier its rival – including by a menacing publicity campaign – the trial observed due constitutional process. The Republic's political culture remained democratic against all the odds.

The Ebro offensive, without which the POUM trial cannot properly be understood, was also the Republic's last throw of the dice. It had three objectives: to protect Valencia from Francoist conquest (first attempted by Italian forces); to restore contact with Catalonia, thus reuniting the two Republican zones; and thirdly to demonstrate to an international audience the resilience of the Republican army and its capacity to plan and implement offensive action. British Foreign Office opinion noted at the end of 1938 that 'the Ebro campaign was without any doubt a great [Republican] Government victory'. It also noted that Franco was more heavily reliant than ever on Italy and Germany. This was especially true in terms of airpower. The Ebro saw massive air battles that were unprecedented in the history of warfare and would not be seen again until the Battle of Britain in the opening stages of the Second World War.

Franco paid Nazi Germany in mining rights to guarantee his air superiority at the Ebro. Whatever his assurances to British diplomats in 1936 that this would not happen, by 1938 Franco's desperate need for more airpower to win the war meant he was prepared to cede what he had previously resisted. The product of these valuable mineral concessions played a vital part in Germany's re-armament programme. But the military advantage Franco gained paid immense dividends in the short term. Republican communications were bombed to oblivion and, as so many international brigader memoirs testify, their troops were blasted off the bare and rocky hillsides by the sheer force of the incendiary materiel launched.

In military terms, all the intervening powers were keen to use the opportunity provided by the Spanish war to train their personnel and to test equipment and strategies in real and extended combat conditions – although these were collateral benefits rather than motives for their initial intervention. Germany and Russia welcomed the chance to try out new technology – above all against the other, understood as the eventual 'territorial' opponent. So it was that in Spain elements of what would become *Blitzkrieg* made their appearance, while the Soviet Union benefited especially from being able to test its tanks and armoured cars. But it was the war in the air – in which nearly 3,000 planes participated – that really marked Spain out in terms of technical and technological innovation (for example, the precision bombing of specific targets or new techniques for dealing with anti-aircraft fire).

In the end, in November 1938, the Republican forces had to retreat back across the River Ebro, which they had crossed with such feats of engineering ingenuity, improvisation, and tenacity the previous July. The usual problems obtained due to shortages of materiel and reserves. But at the Ebro there was a huge difference. This time the retreat was a function not of military defeat (the Republic had successfully blocked Franco's attack on Valencia), but of an absolutely devastating political defeat that occurred many miles from Spain.

At the end of September 1938, in Munich, Britain and France signed an agreement with the German and Italian dictatorships that effectively gave Hitler the green light to invade and dismember Czechoslovakia, the one remaining functioning democracy in central and eastern Europe. In signing away Czech independence, the Western democracies also killed the Spanish Republic. For Munich demonstrated their apparently unbreakable commitment to appeasing the fascist powers, and the resulting diplomatic impasse fatally undermined both Negrín's resistance strategy and his personal political credibility in the eyes of many of his desperate and war-weary compatriots. Munich was almost certainly also the key event determining the reconfiguration of Soviet foreign policy that would eventually lead to the Nazi-Soviet 'non-aggression' pact of August 1939.

Demoralization induced by the now utterly bleak international horizon partly explains the rapidity of Catalonia's fall in February 1939. What Franco's bombing raids had failed to achieve was brought about by the cumulative effects of Non-Interventionist embargo and the Republic's near total diplomatic isolation. As one witness recalled, people started to wish for the end: 'just let it be over, it doesn't matter how it ends, but let it end now'. As Franco's troops closed in on Catalonia in February, hundreds of thousands of refugees streamed across the border into French internment camps.

After the fall of Catalonia, Negrín's plan was to defend at least some part of the centre-south zone in an indefinite holding action until the international situation broke – a strategy which at the very least would have permitted a process of controlled withdrawal and the evacuation of those most at risk – as the need arose. Negrín understood what few other Republican leaders did: that only continued residual resistance could give them a bargaining chip with Franco and his backers. Once the Republicans had laid down their arms, then Franco would not negotiate anything.

For the *Generalísimo*, in accordance with his political war aims, was interested in only one route to 'peace': that of unconditional Republican surrender. In February 1939, he published the terms of the scarifying (and retroactive) Law of Political Responsibilities, which would allow the regime to implement blanket repression, and whose publication at this point was itself an act of war. Most ominously, the Law constituted Franco's ringing negative reply to Negrín's last non-negotiable condition for a ceasefire: a guarantee of no reprisals against the defeated Republican population. This, post-Munich, had in fact been Negrín's only non-negotiable condition to end the war.

But the implications of Munich spurred on other republican and socialist leaders. Made mad by desperation, they still believed, against all the evidence and odds, in the chimera of a negotiated peace with Franco. In March 1939, their activities combined with massive war-weariness in Republican territory to spark a complex political and social rebellion in Madrid against the Negrín government and the Spanish Communist Party, the forces symbolizing continued resistance. It was then that the heterogeneity of communist mobilization in wartime Spain became the party's Achilles' heel, as professional army officers in the centre zone who were members of the party refused to obey its orders to continue resisting. It was, thus, the political implosion of the Republic rather than outright military defeat that afforded Franco's forces their victory in the war.

This political implosion once again reveals as fantastical the claims about Republican 'Sovietization'. Such claims stem anyway from a deeply anachronistic reading of history – namely that the Soviet Union intervening in Spain in 1936 was already the political and economic superpower of the post-Second World War period. Even after 1945, satellitization still required some preconditions: geographical proximity and the red army for sure and, preferably, a partially shared political culture. In Spain none of these things obtained. Nothwithstanding the growth of the Spanish communist movement during the war, there remained between the Republican political class and the Soviet cupola a veritable abyss which no amount of measured diplomatic or political exchange could bridge. The communist movement itself was, moreover, atypically heterogeneous. Most tellingly of all, as we have just seen, in Spain there was no equivalent of a 'red army'.

The populous and territorially substantial Republican centre-south zone, with the capital city of Madrid, was never captured militarily by Franco. It was surrendered by the commanding officers of the defending armies in the political and diplomatic impasse of late March 1939. The major part played in the hand-over by the forces of a well-organized fifth column, which turned out to have had excellent communications with the besieging forces, raises so far unanswered questions about the role it played in the anti-Negrín rebellion that capsized Republican resistance. In the panic and confusion, the Republican fleet set sail from Cartagena, fetching up at Bizerta in North Africa, where it was interned by the French authorities pending delivery to Franco. The thousands of Republican refugees thronging Valencia, Alicante, Gandía, and other ports on Spain's east (Levante) coast had lost their only viable means of escape from the centre-south zone, bounded by hostile territory and the sea. A minority escaped on other vessels – mostly those who had money to pay a passage. Among the majority left behind, some committed suicide. The rest were herded into the concentration camps set up by the conquering Francoist forces. With Spanish Republican defeat, Nazi firepower was now freed up for other colonial ventures in Europe.

In early January 1937, when Goering met Mussolini in Rome, the German leader had commented that they had at most three weeks. If Italy and Germany could not secure a victory for Franco in that time, then it would all be over, because after that the British would be bound to wake up and stop them. Negrín never ceased believing that sooner or later Britain and France would have to wake up and stop appeasing Germany and Italy if they wanted to retain their imperial advantage – or even out of sheer survival instinct. Once that happened, then even the least favourable scenario would mean that Franco's backers would no longer be able to maintain their support and he would thus have no option but to negotiate with the Republic. That was why Negrín went on resisting. If Britain and France had heeded him, then the whole course of European history might have been different – *Anschluss*, Munich, even the Second World War itself. But historians cannot deal in counter-factual speculation, however compelling. What is demonstrably the case is that Franco did Hitler the colossal service of altering the European balance of power in favour of the German-Italian Axis, while Spanish Republican resistance, achieved for nearly three years in the teeth of British policy, actively delayed other forms of Nazi aggression in Europe and, in so doing, made Britain itself a priceless gift of time to re-arm.

Chapter 6
Victory and defeat: the wars after the war

Franco's victory in the Civil War meant the beginning of an attempt to achieve economic modernization in Spain without the accompanying products of 'modernity': the mass political democracy and cultural pluralism symbolized by the Republic. Over 400,000 Spaniards sought sanctuary in exile. Some achieved the relative safety of Mexico and the Americas. But thousands of others were sucked straight into the European maelstrom of war and annihilation.

The other fronts of Republican Spain

> . . . a lone soldier, carrying the flag of a country that is not his own, of a country that is all countries and which only exists because that soldier raises its abolished flag . . . ragged, dusty and anonymous, a tiny figure in that blazing sea of infinite sand, walking onwards . . . not really knowing where he's going nor with whom, nor why, not really caring as long as it's onwards, onwards, always onwards.
>
> (Javier Cercas, *Soldados de Salamina*)

The Republican soldiers and civilians who crossed the frontier from Catalonia to France in February 1939 were immediately detained by the hostile authorities in internment 'camps' where the lack of sanitation and shelter caused ravages among inmates already weakened by the privations of war. Interned alongside the Spanish

19. Franco's victory parade in Madrid

Republicans were international brigaders who could not return to their countries of origin. Those who could escaped. As political refugees, the choices for both Republicans and brigaders were stark and brutal. The Popular Front was dead in France as well as Spain and the Daladier government viewed them with suspicion and distaste. Great efforts were made to achieve the Spanish refugees' voluntary repatriation, an option taken by approximately 70,000 by March 1939. After a few months, and with women and children decanted elsewhere, the remaining active male population of the French camps was given the option of continued internment or release into the Foreign Legion, the *Bataillons de marche* (a kind of quarantined conscription), or deployment in semi-militarized work brigades. Of the 60,000 who left the camps (over 100,000 remained), most chose the work brigades, and of these a majority were sent to north-eastern France to fortify the Maginot Line. There Republicans from the work brigades fought the German invasion in May–June 1940, and it was along the lines of retreat that they carried out their first acts of resistance as sabotage against the occupying forces.

Some Republicans passed directly to forms of clandestine resistance. Others joined later as escapees from camps where they had been re-interned. Though this was much harder by the winter of 1940, when many more Republican veterans (including international brigaders) were held under the harsh regime of the penal camps of Gurs and Vernet d'Ariège, from where some would also be dispatched to North African concentration camps. Others were now in prisoner-of-war camps (stalags), where the Nazis initially confined those Spanish Republicans they captured fighting with the French army. Spaniards deployed in Vichy's foreign labour detachments and other forms of rural public and forestry works were soon involved in sabotage. For most Republican refugees in France, the roads to resistance began with the imperatives of survival in everyday life. They figured large among the class of 'irregular civilians', as one historian of the Resistance has called them. Desperate to avoid internment or repatriation, Republicans

20. Republican refugee camp in south-western France, March 1939. (There were several. Pictured is either Argelès-sur-Mer or Le Barcarès.)

existed on the social and economic margins doing their utmost to avoid the attention of Vichy officials and occupying forces. To help each other survive, they created solidarity networks that would in time become networks of resistance. The precariousness of refugee lives meant that Republicans learned through experience that there was often no clear dividing line between survival and resistance. But among those engaged in active resistance there was also a strong awareness that by defending France's Republican tradition they were continuing the collective struggle necessarily left behind in Spain in February 1939.

The *maquis*, in its incipient stages in 1941 in the south-west of France, grew out of the practical military knowledge, skills, and experience of Spanish Republican veterans. They were the ones who knew the techniques of sabotage – how to make bombs out of scraps, lay an ambush, or derail a train without using explosives. Women too were involved, frequently undertaking crucial and highly dangerous liaison work. Republicans were also integral to the underground networks that supported Allied counter-intelligence and organized escape routes between France and Spain. These operated in both directions, evacuating Allied military personnel and endangered civilians as well as bringing in Allied agents and Republican refugees in danger of detention or worse by the Franco regime. One of those involved in liaison work was Neus Català, the daughter of tenant farmers in Tarragona and a member of the Catalan Communist Party. In February 1944, she would be deported to Ravensbrück in the largest convoy of women ever sent from France, among whom were some 27 Spanish Republicans. Català survived and after the war gathered scores of testimonies and commemorations from other Republican women resisters and deportees. But it would take another 40 years – until the end of Francoism – before her book could be published in Spain.

From late 1942, the consequences of Nazi occupation, and in particular forced labour policies, began to stimulate large-scale resistance in Europe. Accordingly, the Spanish Republican *maquis* became part of multiform and expanding rural and urban resistance movements across France. The Spaniards who fought in the *maquis* in France were waging the same irregular war of sabotage, propaganda, and survival as their fellow Republicans who had stayed behind in Spain as an indigenous guerrilla fighting Franco's security forces. Whether they had remained through choice or necessity, the Republican *maquis* in Spain understood their own struggle as another front in the war of resistance emerging across Europe by 1943 to the brutal forms of racial, ethnic, and social classification espoused by the Nazis and their collaborators.

Nowhere was the murderousness of Hitler's new order more apparent than on the Eastern Front, where Spanish Republicans also fought against the German armies. Ironically, some had originally been evacuated as young people from the war-torn north of Spain in 1937 and sent to the Soviet Union (among other destinations) to protect them from the massive aerial bombing then being inflicted on Republican cities by Franco's Nazi and Fascist backers. There were about 3,000 child refugees from Republican Spain in the Soviet Union. Some 2,000 adults came later, mainly in the diaspora of 1939. These were mostly military and political personnel connected to the Spanish communist movement. All, without exception, were flung into the Soviet Union's vast and harsh industrial mobilization for war following the German invasion of June 1941. Those Republicans who served as combatants did so mainly in guerrilla units, a few were pilots, and other Republican men and women served as soldiers and nurses in the defence of Leningrad and Moscow. They also fought and died at Stalingrad. Of some 700 Republican combatants on the Eastern Front, about 300 were killed, including the only sons of Republican Spain's two pre-eminent women politicians: the iconic communist leader Dolores Ibárruri (Pasionaria), whose 22-year-old son Rubén died at Stalingrad in September 1942, and Margarita Nelken, the art critic, writer, social reformer, and parliamentary champion of Spain's landless poor, whose son Santiago was killed in action in the Ukraine in January 1944, also aged 22.

The continuing struggle for Spanish Republican democracy was evident on every front, including in Africa. When France fell in June 1940, more than 2,000 Spanish Republican veterans found themselves scattered with French forces in colonial and dependent territories from Syria to the Maghreb. Some 300 of these Republicans were already veterans of April's Anglo-French action at Narvik (Norway), where the all-Spanish 13th Semi-Brigade of the French Foreign Legion had acted as shock troops, sustaining appallingly high casualties in consequence. When most of the French authorities in the Maghreb accepted the authority of Vichy, most Republican veterans who could rallied to De Gaulle's French forces. For some, this involved crossing the Sahara Desert from Morocco and Algeria all the way to Chad in French Equatorial Africa in order to enlist in General Leclerc's 2nd Armoured Division. This force fought in Libya and then alongside the British 8th Army elsewhere in North Africa. After taking part in the Normandy landings, Leclerc's division would be the first Allied contingent to enter Paris, in August 1944.

The Republicans fighting with Leclerc's forces named their tanks 'Guadalajara', 'Brunete', 'Belchite', 'Ebro', and 'Madrid' after Civil War battles and places to which one day they hoped for the exile's return. They considered themselves fortunate to be able to fight given that many of their comrades languished or had already died in Vichy's North African concentration camps. Still others endured desperate conditions in its forced labour brigades, including those being used to build the trans-Saharan railway. There they worked with other European refugees from fascism who had enlisted in the Foreign Legion, like the Spanish Republicans, as an explicit means of fighting the Nazis' new order.

> . . . with five other men from the Foreign Legion . . . Miralles . . . the
> [Spanish Republican] veteran of all the wars . . . took part in the

attack on the Italian oasis of Murzak, in south west Libya [in January 1941]. . . . 'Just imagine . . . ' said Bolaño . . . as if he were himself discovering the story, or the meaning of the story, as he told it. 'All of Europe controlled by the Nazis, and in middle of nowhere, without anyone knowing it, there they damn well were – four North Africans, a black guy and that old cuss of a Spaniard . . . raising the flag of freedom for the first time in months.'

The heterogenous ethnic composition of the free French forces, underscored here in Javier Cercas' epochal best-selling Spanish novel, *Soldados de Salamina* (*Soldiers of Salamis*), thus becomes central to the meaning of the war. Miralles, the 'veteran of all the wars', and Cercas' fictional participant in the real desert odyssey of Spanish Republicans from the Maghreb via Chad to Libya, is one of Hitler and Franco's mongrel soldiers who with their anti-heroism save Europe from fascism's idealization of racial purity and martial virtue. In the novel they 'volunteer' for Murzak by dint of drawing lots and losing. Their own 'virtue' is born of pragmatism and contingency, called into being only to oppose the deathly purity and brutal categorization against which they fight. In the process, as Cercas' novel underlines, it was they, not their Spengler-quoting opponents, who were the soldiers saving civilization at the eleventh hour.

In metropolitan France too, the energy of 'red' Spaniards, as the Nazis and the Francoists both called them, constituted a driving force in the resistance movements in the south and the north. Highly influential in the southern zone of France was the important XIVth Corps of the Spanish Republican Army. During the Civil War it had waged innovative guerrilla and commando-based warfare on a scale that archival research is only now bringing to light. By the autumn of 1943, the XIVth Corps was more or less assimilated to the *Franc-tireurs et partisans* (FTP), a major axis of the French Resistance. Closely allied to the FTP was the urban-based MOI (*Main d'oeuvre immigrée*, or migrant labour front), whose cultural cosmopolitanism and racial heterogeneity as much as its political radicalism made it the living antithesis of Hitler's new order.

The MOI traced its origins to International Brigade veterans – mainly escapees from the prison camp of Gurs – and to the tradition of left internationalism that had underwritten their involvement in the Spanish Civil War. As well as French and Spanish Republican fighters, MOI included Italians, Romanians, Armenians, Poles, Austrians, Czechs, and Hungarians. As in the International Brigades themselves, so too in the MOI, a great many, perhaps more than half, were Jewish. This profile put the MOI under greater psychological pressure than any other resistance organization. Not only were the risks already greater in an urban environment, but a majority of its members were on the wanted list three times over: as leftists, as foreigners, and as Jews. The execution of 22 MOI fighters – several of whom had fought in Spain – in February 1944, after the organization had inflicted some serious losses on the occupying forces in Paris, gave rise to the famous 'Red poster', hundreds of copies of which the Nazis plastered over the walls of the city (see Figure 21). (The 23rd member of the MOI condemned to death was a Romanian woman, Olga Bancic, who was executed in Germany a few months later.)

The attempt in the poster to delegitimize the resistance though an appeal to French chauvinism now documents something else entirely: that the war against the new order was a civil war within, as well as between, European countries, and a war whose significance was literally embodied in the multi-ethnic and cosmopolitan resisters who waged it. From 1943, the FTP in Paris was also led by two other Spanish Civil War veterans, including the French brigader Henri Rol-Tanguy, whose Resistance *nom de guerre* 'Rol' derived from the second surname he had adopted in 1938 in memory of a comrade killed at the battle of the Ebro.

It was to a Spanish Republican unit too that General Leclerc granted the honour of vanguard position in the liberation of Paris.

21. The famous 'Red poster' produced by the Nazis shows the faces of 10 of the 22 FTP-MOI resistance fighters captured and executed in Paris in February 1944. Many in the MOI's founding cadres were International Brigader and Republican escapees from the Gurs prison camp. Three of the 10 pictured here had fought for the Republic in Spain: Celestino Alonso, Shloime Grzywacz, and Francisc Wolf, whose *nom de guerre* was Joseph Boczoř.

This was partly in recognition of the Spanish contribution to the resistance – more than 10,000 urban and rural fighters by 1944 – but also because 'Paris' signified the symbolic antechamber to the liberation of Madrid where, so the exiles fervently hoped, Allied troops would finish the job started by the guerrilla. But in the space of less than a year the Republicans would have definitively lost the battle for Madrid. The Allied liberation of Europe stopped at the Pyrenees. In the autumn of 1944, Republican veterans were left to go it alone across the frontier, where they were inevitably routed by Franco's forces and pushed back to France into what, this time, would be a definitive exile. Hitler was defeated in 1945. But Franco was well on the way to winning the Second World War. His dictatorship would be left in place by Western powers increasingly preoccupied with Cold War divisions and prepared to turn a blind eye to mass killing and repression inside Spain in return for Franco's repeated affirmation of crusading anti-communism.

This blind eye was turned in spite of the fact that Spain had functioned as a valuable Axis resource virtually throughout the Second World War, for all its formal status as a non-belligerent. Indeed, its value to Hitler derived precisely from that status. Franco, who did not break off diplomatic relations with the Third Reich until VE day on 8 May 1945, provided Hitler with stategic raw materials, food, and labour. He also allowed the refuelling and supplying of U-boats, provided Germany with radar, air reconnaissance, and espionage facilities within Spain and access to Spanish propaganda services in Latin America. This assistance stemmed from a deep ideological affinity between Francoist Spain and Nazi Germany. This was manifest in the Gestapo's strong influence over the Spanish police apparatus and in the way the Falangist press was permitted to relay Nazi propaganda material as if it were news. The best-known consequence of the affinity, however, was the dispatch in 1941 of the Falangist Blue Division, as a result of which some 47,000 Spanish troops would fight with the armies of the Third Reich on the Eastern Front. A less well-known consequence was Franco's complaisance in allowing the Nazis to strip prisoner-of-war status from the thousands of Spanish Republican prisoners in their power, thus permitting them to be sent from the stalags to concentration camps.

It was the Franco regime's refusal to recognize the prisoners' Spanish nationality that opened the way to deportation. Indeed, the Nazi authorities announced their policy on 25 September 1940, during the visit to Germany of Franco's second-in-command, Ramón Serrano Suñer, the Spanish Interior (and by October 1940 also Foreign) Minister who was also head of the fascist single party, the Falange. Republican Spaniards were subsequently confined in many different concentration camps: Dachau, Oranienburg, Buchenwald, Flossenburg, Ravensbrück, Auschwitz, Bergen-Belsen, Neuengamme, and, above all, Mauthausen. Most of the Republican prisoners bore on their camp uniforms the blue triangle of the stateless. But some had the red triangle denoting political deportees, notoriously classified by the Nazi bureaucracy as *Nacht und Nebel*: prisoners whose active anti-fascism condemned them to explicit obliteration, as if into the 'night and fog' of Wagnerian allusion for which the policy was named.

Around 10,000 Spanish Republicans died in Nazi camps – which is as many, if not more, than the number who died fighting in the Second World War (the latter figure is notoriously difficult to calculate; estimates – covering both uniformed fighters and irregular combatants – vary from 6,000 to 10,000). Some, like Diego Morales, another veteran of all the wars, survived even the war that was Buchenwald, only to die 'stupidly' of dysentery as the camp was liberated. We know of Morales because he is recalled in an incandescent memoir, *L'ecriture ou la vie* (*Literature or Life*), by his resistance comrade and fellow deportee, Jorge Semprún. The son of a Spanish Republican diplomat, Semprún survived the deportation to become a leader of the underground resistance to Franco in the 1950s and early 1960s, and, much later, Minister of

Culture in Spain's social democratic government. In his work, and supremely in *Literature or Life*, Semprún has given us some of the most remarkable writing we possess on the meaning of the camps in European culture and memory. Semprún chose to write in French because for him Castilian Spanish had become a language occupied by the political and cultural enemy.

Of all the camps, Mauthausen was the Republicans' own particular heart of darkness: 7,200 were incarcerated there, of whom 5,000 died – half of all the Spaniards who perished in Nazi camps. Mauthausen is also a camp for which an exceptional visual record survives: photographs taken mainly by the camp authorities. As the war turned inexorably against Germany, the order was issued for them to be destroyed, but a considerable number were spirited away by a group of Republican prisoners, including two Catalans, Antonio García and Francisco Boix. The young Boix, who as a 16-year-old in 1936 Barcelona had photographed the energy and hopeful mobilization of the socialist and communist youth to which he belonged, managed at the beginning of 1945, through the solidarity network within the camp, to smuggle out a large quantity of pictures with a group of teenage Spanish inmates who were hired to work in a private quarry in the village of Mauthausen.

There the photographs were hidden by a woman called Anna Pointner, who had connections to the Austrian socialist movement and whose garden backed onto the quarry. When the camp was liberated in May, Boix recouped the pictures en route to Paris. Constituting a unique record in both quantity and quality, the photographs were later used in evidence at Nuremberg, before which tribunal Boix himself testified. Of the photographs originally preserved by the camp inmates, about 1,000 remain today. After the war, Boix worked as a news photographer in France, but he was dogged by illness, his health ruined by the camp. In 1951, at the age of 30, he died of acute kidney failure – one of many other 'stupid' deaths, in Semprún's wracking idiom.

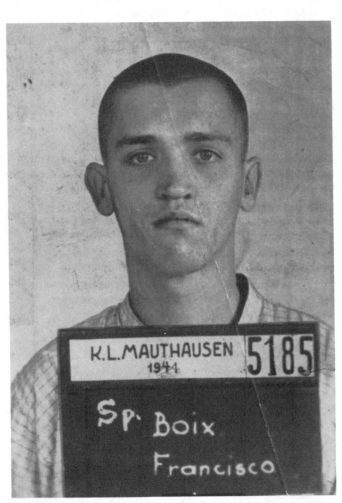

22. Francisco Boix, the teenager who in 1937 had taken his camera with him to the front in Spain, was deported from a stalag to Mauthausen concentration camp in 1941 and there appointed official camp photographer. Boix had been captured as part of a French work brigade from which friends had tried in vain to procure his release.

Franco's Volksgemeinschaft

Aquí la flama de l'esperit és un record vague, una història perduda

(Here the spark of human spirit is a dim memory, a lost history)
(Agustí Bartra, Tercera elegia)

In this place nothing belongs to you
(Warder, Les Corts Prison, Barcelona, 1942)

The space of the camp and of 'war without limit' also existed inside Spain. Francisco Boix's own father died in political incarceration there in 1942. Like the Nazi new order of which it aspired to be a part, Francoist Spain too was to be constructed as a monolithic community by means of the brutal exclusion of specific categories of people.

Those excluded, broadly speaking, were defeated Republican constituencies who could not leave Spain: urban workers, the rural landless, regional nationalists, liberal professionals, and 'new' women – groups that had challenged the established order culturally, politically, or economically. For the Franco regime they were all 'reds' and, once placed beyond the nation, they were deemed to be without rights.

Tens of thousands were executed – judicially murdered after summary military trials. Hundreds of thousands more men, women, and children spent time in what historians now term 'the penal universe' of Francoism: reformatories and prisons, concentration camps and forced labour battalions, where the military forces detached to organize these referred to themselves as 'the army of occupation'. Those confined were subject to a sustained and brutal attempt to reconfigure their consciousness and values. To this end, tens of thousands found themselves coerced, maltreated, and humiliated on a daily basis. Sometimes, however, the pressure applied was even greater. Matilde Landa, a

23. Republican political prisoners in gaol in Spain, 1952 (penal de Ocaña)

leading political activist whose death sentence was commuted to life imprisonment in 1939, used her experience of the law to establish one of the first legal aid services for her fellow prisoners. Partly because she was famous and partly because she was an educated woman of 'good' birth, and thus deemed 'recuperable' according to regime tenets, huge efforts were exerted to make her repudiate her political views and to accept baptism and confession. She was even promised her freedom in return for a public 'recantation'. When this failed, Landa was repeatedly held in solitary confinement for longer and longer periods of time. Transferred from Madrid to the women's gaol in Palma de Mallorca, where the coercion continued, Matilde Landa fell to her death from an internal prison window on 26 September 1942 in what may have been suicide.

Among the other victims of the Francoist worldview were the 'lost children'. These were the babies and young children who, after being removed from their imprisoned mothers, had their names changed so they could be adopted by regime families. Many thousands of working-class children were also sent to state institutions because the authorities considered their own Republican families 'unfit' to raise them. The Franco regime spoke of the 'protection of minors'. But this idea of protection was integrally linked to regime discourses of punishment and purification. In theory, the punishment was of the parents, the 'redemption', or 'rehabilitation', of the children. But the reality, as experienced by Republican children, was of an ingrained belief in state personnel (religious in particular, but others too) that the children had actively to *expiate* the 'sins of the fathers'. Yet, at the same time, the children were repeatedly told that they too were irrecuperable. As such, they were frequently segregated from other classes of inmate in state institutions and mistreated both physically and mentally in other ways.

One child who endured both a Nazi concentration camp and a Francoist reformatory in 1940s Barcelona has written of their fundamental institutional similarities as factories of dehumanization, while another 'lost child' of the Francoist institutions, interviewed in his 70s for a television documentary, spoke of the 'real him' as having died during his incarceration in the 1940s. His comment eerily evokes the idea of the concentration camp *revenant*. As Jorge Semprún remarked, one did not 'return' from the camps, except as a ghost.

Work too in 1940s Spain was presented as a way that the sinful could redeem themselves. Republican prisoners became slave labourers: 20,000 worked to hew out of sheer rock the basilica known as the Valley of the Fallen (*Valle de los Caídos*), Franco's monument to his victorious crusade and the winning side in the Civil War. Republican labour battalions were also used by the army and hired out to private enterprise. The state agency responsible for overseeing them was called the committee for the *redemption* of prison sentences through work. Catholic notions of penitence and expiation through suffering were here permitting extreme economic exploitation.

Those most heavily targeted by the regime's penal discipline were, unsurprisingly, urban workers – the Republican social constituency *par excellence*, now made prostrate by defeat. Historians may debate whether a victorious Republic could have retained worker support in spite of the harsh economic consequences of peacetime reconstruction. What is certain is that the Franco regime never faced this problem. In overtly excluding huge numbers of urban and rural workers from its definition of the national community, it acquired an ideological justification for their economic exploitation in the name of 'national rebirth'. The sub-subsistence wages thus justified were a crucial factor in the accelerated accumulation of profits by banks, industry, and big landowners across the 1940s. Repression would play an important part in the economic boom of the 1960s too, by guaranteeing the 'stability' that made Spain attractive to foreign investors.

Nor was social exclusion under Franco class-specific. Extensive purges among the civil service, and especially of university and school teachers, meant substantial numbers of Spain's professional middle classes joined the ranks of the excluded. Elements of cultural repression were particularly evident in the Basque Country and, above all, in Catalonia, where popular political movements had challenged the concept of an ultra-centralized, Castilianized state. For a time there were bans on the use of the Basque and Catalan languages. In Spain overall, a quarter of all teachers lost the right to exercise their profession. Republicans were also subject to internal exile and their children excluded from university. For example, although Magdalena Maes came from an affluent middle-class family in Zamora, the fact that she was also the niece of Amparo Barayón (whose extra-judicial murder was discussed in Chapter 2) meant Magdalena was unable to study or pursue her chosen career of journalism.

For the civil dead, the war would continue across the 1940s in many intense forms of institutionalized repression and discrimination through which the regime was constructed. No sphere was immune from Francoist ideological mobilization: work/employment and education, as we have seen, but also the law, economy, culture, the very organization of everyday life and public space. Through all these channels, the regime was actively engaged in building up a manichaean division of Spaniards into victors and vanquished.

History itself became a weapon in this work of exclusion. Franco legitimized his violent new order by reference to an ultra-conservative reading of Spanish history – one that had, significantly, been challenged under the Republic. He erected a repressive myth of a monolithic Spanish 'nation' born in the 15th century with the Catholic Kings, where hierarchy and cultural homogeneity, guaranteed by integrist Catholicism, had generated imperial greatness. Although the empire was gone, metropolitan Spain under Franco would be great again as a bulwark against the 'sins' of modernity epitomized by the Republic: enlightenment freethinking, the acceptance of levelling change, and a tolerance of cultural difference/heterogeneity.

The regime instituted the *Causa General*, a sort of untruth and non-reconciliation commission before whose tribunals across Spain testimony was invited on 'red crimes'. Those who testified, having lost loved ones – including in the extra-judicial killings that followed in the wake of the July 1936 military coup – almost certainly derived closure and some measure of solace from the proceedings. But the lack of evidential guarantees (including sometimes the crude fabrication of evidence), and the emphasis on lurid denunciation, underscored the main object of the proceedings as the legitimation and stabilization of the regime through the creation of a manichaean narrative of the Civil War. The main message of the *Causa General* was that atrocities had been committed only by Republicans and endured only by Franco supporters. Those denounced could find themselves, if apprehended, subject to judicial process in a system in which the law itself was operating as a major instrument of repression.

Until 1963 all defendants deemed to be opponents of the Francoist order were brought before military courts. The civil justice system continued to exist and to play a complementary role in the repression. But military judges were appointed to its courts, and its jurisdiction was further curtailed by the creation of numerous special sections whose purpose was also predominantly repressive. Most notable here were the Tribunal for the Eradication of Freemasonry and Communism (1940) and the Law of Political Responsibilities (1939), a piece of catch-all, retrospective legislation (it could be applied back to October 1934) that epitomized bad legal practice and the Franco regime's vengeful dynamic. The law allowed economic tribute to be exacted in fines and expropriations from defendants and their families. Those sentenced by military courts were also automatically referred to the Political Responsibilities tribunals. But many who came before the latter were penalized not for what they had done, but rather for acts of omission: that is, for not having actively supported the military rebellion. As many as 500,000 people were subject to Political Responsibilities proceedings between 1939 and 1945 and, although tens of thousands of these cases never reached the sentencing stage – often through bureaucratic backlog and a lack of state personnel – the repressive effects on those arraigned were scarcely lessened for this.

In other ways too, Francoist legal decisions wrecked lives. Perhaps one of the most traumatic but least discussed was the reversal of Republican divorce and marriage legislation (which also made children illegitimate). Not only were divorces retroactively unmade, but those who had married in civil ceremonies were obliged to re-marry in church if they wanted their status to be recognized. But priests would frequently refuse – if they disapproved of the politics or ethics of either of the parties. In this and other ways, Church personnel were major agents of social discipline in post-war Spain, reflecting the institutional alliance of Church and state that was so crucial to the political legitimation of Francoism. An integral part of this arrangement was that priests reported on their parishioners to the political authorities, denouncing 'reds' to state tribunals.

Denunciation was a major mechanism to trigger the detention and trial of Republicans in post-war Spain. But priests were not the only denouncers. Tens of thousands of ordinary Spaniards also responded to the regime's enthusiastic encouragement – out of political conviction, social prejudice, opportunism, or fear. They denounced their neighbours, acquaintances, and even family members – denunciations for which no corroboration was either sought or required. Even though the system itself was instigated by the regime, the consequences of denunciation created dense webs of complicity and collaboration. In other words, the work of legitimating Francoism and building its brutal community was occurring deep inside Spanish society. This happened in other ways too – through the everyday humiliations that taught the defeated the lessons of power and the meaning of their defeat. When, for example, a 'red' father had to go cap in hand to neighbours known to have good connections to the regime in order to get help for a sick child.

These moments of interaction were central to how power was reconstructed and local (and thus national) hierarchies rebuilt. But Spain in the immediate post-war period remained a place of frighteningly separate social worlds. Alongside savage poverty and widespread terror, there existed other milieux of ease, security, and order regained. As Republican women were shaved and dosed with castor oil by the 'victors' of their villages, or transported with their children across Spain in cattletrucks, or raped in police stations, women of the southern landed aristocracy or from affluent provincial middle-class families in Spain's conservative heartland celebrated the redemption of their private family sphere and revelled in the upsurge of public Catholic ceremonial. As one woman who had been close to the conservative Catholic party, CEDA, commented resonantly many decades later:

there was an absence of freedom, but logically for those of us who had well-ordered lives, those of us who were professionals and saw things from the personal viewpoint only, we felt very much at ease and happy.

For the defeated, however, a retreat into the private was rarely possible. To the insecurity of public spaces – on the streets Falangists regularly forced passers-by considered 'dubious' to make the fascist salute – was added the insecurity and fragility of 'home'. More often than not it was empty, as women worked long hours or visited imprisoned family members or sought the means of obtaining scarce supplies of food, often via the black market whose workings further penalized the urban poor. And even when they were 'home', then this was a space increasingly penetrated by state agencies – most notably the women's section of the single state party, Falange – offering low-level welfare services in return for the right to exercise moral supervision and monitor the 'penitence' of the defeated.

Spain's brutal national community was not to be overturned rapidly. By 1945, it was true that the frenzy of killing was diminishing. Franco may have felt the need to exercise some strategic caution in the wake of Axis defeat. But much more importantly, by then the investment of terror had already been made. Moreover, the form in which the Allies chose to penalize the Franco regime for its Axis dalliance – that is, by excluding it from Marshall aid for European reconstruction – also had the material effect of punishing most those who had lost the Civil War. For as the intelligent and far-sighted Republican prime minister Juan Negrín argued forcefully from exile, Spain's inclusion in the Marshall Plan could have mitigated or even undermined the punitive effects of Franco's disciplinary project. Later developments indicate the rightness of his thinking. For it was the labour mobility generated in the 1950s, once Spain's economy had been kick-started by trade and aid agreements with the USA – effectively Spain's very own Marshall Plan – that provided a way out from the rigid hierarchies and unforgiving memories of villages and provincial towns for 'red'/defeated constituencies, most frequently in the shape of their sons and daughters. They headed as migrants to the growing cities to become the new workforce of a burgeoning industrial sector. The exodus of the poor from the rural south during these years finally 'solved' the structural problem of mass landlessness that had been at the heart of Spain's social conflict in the 1930s when the Republic had attempted to address it in a more explicitly egalitarian manner.

By the late 1950s and early 1960s, the city offered a relative degree of anonymity and thus freedom of a sort – even if not from economic exploitation. But the cities no more belonged to the defeated than did the villages of deep Spain, for as long as the Franco regime endured there could be no national symbols or any public discourse that reflected their experience. The defeated cast no reflection. No public space was theirs. While the Francoist dead had war memorials and their names carved on churches – *'caídos por Díos y por España'* ('those who fell for God and Spain') – the Republican dead could never be publicly mourned. The defeated were obliged to be complicit in this denial. Women concealed the violent deaths of husbands and fathers from their children in order to protect them physically and psychologically. In villages all over Spain many kept secret lists of the dead. Sisters mentally mapped the location of their murdered brothers, but never spoke of these things. The silent knowledge of unquiet graves necessarily produced a devastating schism between public and private memory in Spain. It was a schism that would long outlive even the Franco regime itself.

Chapter 7
The uses of history

... we can only forget what we have previously known. The first thing we must do, then, is to know.

(Pedro Laín Entralgo)

Never again will a single story be told as though it were the only one.

(John Berger)

For Spaniards, the Civil War remains a political touchstone of huge importance precisely because of the ideological uses to which it was put by the Franco dictatorship. The regime manipulated a monolithic and highly partisan version of the war – always referring to it as the 'crusade' or 'war of national liberation', never as a civil war.

In 1963, as Spain's beaches began to fill up with mass Euro tourism, the regime – which was still executing people for 'war crimes' – celebrated its 'Twenty-five Years of Peace'. Public ceremonial and the millions of posters plastered over walls in towns and villages the length and breadth of the country portrayed the war as one against the hordes of anti-Spain in thrall to the Judaeo-Marxist-Masonic conspiracy, a war for national unity against separatists, of morality against iniquity. So even in the mid-1960s what was being celebrated was not in fact 'peace' but 'victory'. In so doing, the regime sought to stave off most forms of cultural and social *aggiornamento*. In the process, contemporary history – and above all Civil War history – was reduced to a branch of state propaganda: apologia and hagiography written by Francoist policemen, army officers, priests, and state functionaries, for only they were permitted access to the archives and facilities to publish.

Precisely because of this, Anglo-American historical writing on the Spanish Civil War came to exert a great influence in the 1960s and early 1970s. Comprising diplomatic, high political, and economic studies, it focused on the war's rapid internationalization and its implications for the great power politics of the 1930s. Analytical and intellectually rigorous, this work functioned as an antidote to the Franco regime's tendentious production. But it was, by definition, divorced from the empirical base of Spanish archives.

By the later 1970s and early 1980s, new work was appearing – including by Spaniards – as the transition from Franco's dictatorship to a liberal democratic system initiated a slow thaw. This analysed the internal political development of the warring sides in Spain and their relationship to European polarization in the 1930s. Included here were the initial analyses of Francoism in relation to European fascisms, and research on the International Brigades that fought with the Republic – work that is ongoing, in the latter case not least because of the opening of the Moscow archives. Like its predecessors, this work also stood in opposition to acritical Francoist historical writing. Nevertheless, it sometimes also presented ideology in an overly schematic, or two-dimensional, way.

The political opening in Spain in the late 1970s and early 1980s saw the tentative beginnings of archive-based histories of the Civil War – mostly undertaken by new generations of Spaniards. But their promise was at first severely curtailed, ironically, by the politics of the transition itself. The return of democracy had been agreed by the Francoist elites in return for a *de facto* political amnesty, the so-called 'pact of silence'. No one would be called to account legally, nor would there be any equivalent of a truth and reconciliation commission. While this amnesty did not specifically cover the writing of history, in practice for a while it did. The same social fear of a recrudescent civil war, ceaselessly recalled and manipulated by the dictatorship, and present still in the shape of the firepower of the army and civilian extreme Right in the 1970s and early 1980s, was once again self-censoring Spaniards over what could and could not be said publicly about the war.

But the pact of silence was also the inevitable result of the complicity of 'ordinary Spaniards' in the repression, as discussed in Chapter 6. It was about the guilt of the heirs of those who denounced and murdered, as well as the fears of those whose families suffered repression. There was a widespread fear of the consequences of reopening old wounds that the Franco regime had, decade on decade, expressly and explicitly prevented from healing. The disadvantage of the democratic transition's *modus vivendi*, whatever its necessity in other respects, was that those who had been obliged to be silent for nearly 40 years were once again required to accept that there would not be public recognition of their past lives or memories.

Yet one of the most remarkable features of the late 1980s in Spain was the explosion of detailed empirical works of history that have minutely reconstructed the Francoist repression on a province by province basis. By the beginning of the new millennium about 60% of Spain's provinces have been researched to some degree. Here historians have often been obliged to disinter long-forgotten material from local archives in order to recreate a story for which the analagous sources in state repositories no longer exist. For in spite of the Franco regime trumpeting its moral virtue, by the early 1970s it had taken care to destroy much of the centrally held documentary evidence of the repression located in police, judicial, and military archives. (Also of key significance here, but unsusceptible to supplementation by local knowledge, is the denuded state of Spain's Foreign Ministry archive for the period of the Franco-Hitler *entente* of the 1940s.)

This ongoing endeavour by historians constitutes a necessary restitution in the work of collective memory, the telling of all those complex stories that were silenced by dictatorship's monolithic 'truth', exemplified in the *Causa General*, discussed in Chapter 6. Most crucially, it means the public recognition of all the stories that could not surface under the special and precarious circumstances of the democratic transition. This new history of the repression, told with real names, and counting the dead from municipal registers and cemetery lists, is, in a very real sense, the equivalent of war memorials for those who never had them, for those who were not liberated in 1945. Where 'history', in the shape of a Francoist myth, was once an instrument of repression, now the work of independent historians – both amateur and professional – is a pivotal part of reparation and, as such, an act of democratic and constitutional citizenship.

Old memories, new histories

Luckily for you my son, we stopped being afraid a long time ago in Spain.

(Pedro Almodóvar, *Carne Trémula* [*Live Flesh*], 1997)

But for remembrance to happen properly, fear had to be overcome. Since the beginning of the new millennium there has been an explosion of Republican memory with the creation of civil pressure groups, most notably the Association for the Recuperation of Historical Memory (ARMH). It has petitioned for the exhumation from common graves of the remains of those extra-judicially murdered by Franco's forces so they may be identified and reburied by family and friends. The disappeared are estimated to number around 30,000 in total, but only a small proportion – hundreds rather than thousands – are likely to be exhumed. Those that have been include Pilar Espinosa from Candeleda in Avila, whose extra-judicial murder was described in Chapter 2. Since 1936 her remains had lain with those of the two women killed alongside her in an apparently anonymous roadside grave that had in fact been discreetly marked with a small plain stone by other villagers.

The ARMH itself grew out of founder member Emilio Silva's search for his own grandfather, killed in October 1936 by Francoist vigilantes in Priaranza del Bierzo, León, in north-west Spain. Silva's grandmother, although fully aware of the fate of her husband, never told any of her six children what had happened. In Silva's case, as in so many others, it would be the subsequent generation that felt compelled to ask the questions – spurred by their experience of the apparently unfathomable but pervasive sense of mental absence, anguish, and loss attaching to their elders. The 'grandchild's gaze' as one leading Spanish historian has called it, has been crucial in opening up Spain's past. The shallow roadside grave in Priaranza, León, containing the remains of Silva's grandfather and another 13 victims, became the ARMH's flagship case and was taken to the United Nations High Commissioner for Human Rights. As a result, the grave was exhumed in October 2000, and in May 2003 Emilio Silva's grandfather (also called Emilio Silva) became the first victim of Spain's Civil War to have his identity confirmed by a DNA test. For the Silva family, the circle that had opened violently in October 1936 was closed on 18 October 2003 when Emilio Silva and the 'Priaranza 13' were brought home to be buried, with private ceremonies in local cemeteries. A powerful symbolic charge still attaches to bringing the dead back home, because the old remember how the most devastating effect of the war-unleashing military coup of July 1936 was precisely to annihilate 'home' as a safe space.

One memoir in particular, recounting just such an annihilation, has heralded the eruption into the public sphere of these memories of physical and psychological repression. *A Death in Zamora* was written by the North American-raised son of Amparo Barayón, whose story is told in Chapter 2. He had known nothing of his mother before returning to Spain in the late 1980s to uncover the truth about her imprisonment and extra-judicial murder. The book charts an extraordinary odyssey in time, space, and memory. It indicates too how it has been a dynamic emerging from civil society that has powered the commemoration now occurring in Spain in the opening years of the 21st century.

As well as the publication of works of history on the repression, there has also been a flood of popular and journalistic output (including films and documentaries) about prisons, labour battalions, and the anti-Franco guerrilla of the 1940s, which, as discussed previously, saw themselves not in isolation but as a component of the European wars of resistance against the Nazi new order. Most recently (2003) a documentary about the emotive subject of the 'lost children' removed from their Republican families (*Los niños perdidos del franquismo*) drew huge audiences nationwide. This explosion of Republican memory constitutes an outpouring – before the generations who suffered what it remembers pass for good. For the now elderly victims of forced labour or lengthy political imprisonment, the purpose is that what was done to them should be publicly acknowledged before they die. Here, then, the comparison to be made is with Holocaust memory in its broadest sense – in that one of the crucial triggers is the end of biological memory, and the tremendous sense of sadness, loss, and danger that engenders.

For those of subsequent generations too, these same motives in part obtain. The grandchildren, the generation that has predominantly come to ask the questions, have felt able so to do because, unlike many of their own parents' generation, they feel safe – being sufficiently removed from the direct family trauma and the social and political context that generated it. This begins to answer the question of why the 'grandchild's gaze'. But it can only be part of the answer, not least because it does not explain why the retrieval of these painful events should be of such moment to people for whom they are, essentially, 'post-memory': that is, neither directly experienced as events nor even immediate consequences. This question probably lies beyond the remit of this book, since it places Spain in a broader European context of imponderables related to the tremendous upsurge of memory and commemoration in our times. But in Spain, as elsewhere, this near obsession certainly has to do with a subliminal awareness of all that was lost beyond recuperation – through 'purification', genocide, and diaspora – in the wars of mid-20th-century Europe. 'Memory' may thus also serve as a source of consolation in an age when we no longer believe in certain sorts of progress and yet are still strongly bound by a concept of linear time. More positively, the work of restoring historical fragments is a form of solidarity. 'So many friends whom I never knew disappeared in 1945, the year I was born', writes Patrick Modiano in his search for one of the lost that becomes a memorial to them all.

But for all its civil, cultural significance, commemoration in Spain, as elsewhere in Europe, is always in some way about present-day politics too. And in Spain the complex centre–periphery dynamic makes itself felt in the politics of commemoration as in all else. While Spain's centralist conservative Popular Party (PP), in government from March 1996 until March 2004, was reluctant to support any initiative – civil or political – that directly challenged the legitimacy of the Franco regime, Catalan politicians have seen the potential in sponsoring Republican commemorations. In particular, this has enabled Catalan nationalists to question the authenticity of the PP's conversion to an enlightened form of 'constitutional patriotism'. Indeed, the PP's position in the ongoing 'archive wars' would tend to suggest its continued adherence to an older, more aggressively centralist and Castilian-chauvinist conception of patriotism. These archive wars are being waged over documentation that began life as Francoist war booty but now forms part of the holdings of the national Civil War archive in Salamanca (a city that was one of Franco's wartime capitals and which remains the heartland of Catholic, centralist, conservative Spain). While in power, the PP opposed all attempts by the Catalan regional government to have the archive return the originals of

Catalan documentation seized by the advancing Francoist armies during the war and stored in Salamanca so it could be used to incriminate and prosecute the regime's Republican opponents.

Nor has the Catholic Church in Spain yet fully come to terms with its own role in the Francoist repression. In 1971 it issued a public statement which, albeit in very guarded prose, amounted to an apology for the Church's role in the Civil War and its aftermath. By extension, this was also an apology for the crucial contribution the Church had made to legitimizing in the eyes of Western political establishments a dictatorship that had, for more than three decades, daily infringed the basic human rights of Spaniards. But in spite of this, still, in the 21st century, independent historians seeking access to Church sources for the 1940s frequently find their way barred. Indeed, it is ecclesiastical and lay Catholic archives rather than military ones that constitute the final frontier in documenting Spain's Civil War and the ensuing years of uncivil peace.

That the Civil War is still a contested past in Spain is also deducible from many other contemporary symptoms, but none perhaps more evident than the lack of major museum coverage of the war – especially in Madrid. Such representations are much more likely to be found at the periphery – most notably in Guernica in the Basque Country, which has the nearest thing to a modern Civil War exhibition – or else on a small scale as local, temporary exhibitions. By 2003, some exceptions to this have begun to appear in the shape of small, fixed exhibitions, usually in the vicinity of important battle sites, such as, for example, in the village of Morata de Tajuña (Madrid) commemorating the battle of Jarama. But it is significant that these originated in private initiatives. This is true for Catalonia too, even though there such initiatives have subsequently acquired regional government backing.

The Francoist backlash has now also appeared in the form of a popularized history book, Pío Moa's *Los mitos de la guerra civil* (*The Myths of the Civil War*) published in 2003. Its content of anachronistic Francoist propaganda is entirely bankrupt in the face of the past quarter century of national and international historical research. But unlike most of the Spanish publications deriving from this research, *Mitos* is written in a clear and accessible prose style and aimed specifically at a general readership. It has enjoyed an extraordinary commercial success in Spain, including, most notably, among the young, who are vulnerable because coverage of the 1930s and 1940s in school history syllabuses is still frequently patchy or non-existent. The poverty of Moa's work, its inability to convey the complexity and nuanced truth of a past for which many readers are searching, makes it seem anachronistic at a time when the return of Republican memory marks the real coming of age of Spain's democratic culture. But perhaps the Moa phenomenon too is a part of this process – in spite of rather than because of the substance of his work.

The debate around Moa is also occurring within civil society – the very entity the Francoist crusade sought to annihilate. Moa has powerful supporters in the Spanish media, but his unreconstructed Francoism is no longer invested with the power of a repressive state. Spain's civil society is growing stronger and more complex as the campaign around Republican memory and the mass graves indicates. And even Moa has been massively outsold by Javier Cercas' *The Soldiers of Salamis*, a Civil War novel that subtly and humanely debunks the sterile values of Moa's coup-unleashing 'honourable soldiers'. In the end too, even the lack of funds hampering the work of the Association for the Recuperation of Historical Memory may be a price worth paying for its independence. For when governments and states – even if they are liberal democratic ones – promote public remembrance, this changes the meaning and value of such remembrance. Memory work that emanates from civil society is inherently more healing and more useful in terms of building a democratic culture. As the anthropologist Michael Taussig puts it, such work 'allows the moral and magic powers of the unquiet dead to flow into the public sphere'.

Where, then, do present-day agendas of commemoration and contemporary politics, and the increasingly complex mix of the two, leave the historian of Spain's long Civil War? We have seen how, from the early 1990s, work by a new generation of historians inside Spain has come to focus on the war as a conflict involving the whole of society. It has begun by dismantling Francoist myths and successfully so, in spite of Moa's work. There are now also appearing new works that build on social history methodologies developed by other European practitioners. There are still some huge, pivotal topics to be scrutinized here – not least the role of conscription and the army as a source of nation-building, perhaps especially in Republican Spain. And just as other European historians are also now turning to explore the intimate links between mass political mobilization, cultural change, and individual identity/subjectivity in the 1930s, so too in Spain we need to put under the lens the gender and generational revolution that was occurring in people's heads as well as on the streets and which reached its crescendo during the Civil War. But whatever the specific themes, what this work has in common is that it adds to our understanding of the complexity and contradiction of social and cultural change as these were being worked out in wartime Spain.

But for non-Spaniards the idea of the Republican war effort as the 'last great cause' still exercises an enormous attraction. This is the resonant and enduring legacy of the European and American Left. It is often said that the defeat of the Spanish Republic proved a defining moment for progressives. After Spain there could be no 'grand narrative', no belief in history as a force impelling enlightened humanistic change. It is paradoxical then that the 'last great cause' itself has for so long seemed immune to the implications of this realization. In the 1930s the idea encapsulated the overwhelming emotional commitment of many in Europe and beyond to the live political cause of the democratic Republic at war and thus served as an important rallying cry to mobilize practical assistance. In both these senses, we have to understand 'the last great cause' as an historical phenomenon in its own right. But we also need to be wary of using it as an interpretative schema to write the history of the war.

Indeed, in some ways, the 'last great cause' has become, like other enduring but overly simple formulations, such as the 'revolution versus the war', a consolatory story told to mitigate defeat. It also points to the binary worldview that inhabited the culture of the old Left no less than it did its contemporary political opponents – whether Franco in Spain or Joseph McCarthy in the USA. Bill Aalto, the Finnish-American boy from the Bronx who became an international brigader and fought in the Republican guerrilla, was not only a working-class war hero, he was also gay. This was part of the reason why, unlike Irv Goff who had fought alongside him in the guerrilla, Aalto was prevented (by his own comrades) from going back with the Lincolns to fight as part of an American special force alongside the resistance in occupied Europe. Aalto's experience after the Spanish Civil War, the questions he asked about the politics of the personal and the categories of public and private as constructed in the 1940s and 1950s, all foreshadow the emergence of a New Left that was itself a critique of the monolithicity of the old and of its refusal to consider the implications of subjectivity.

The appeal of the 'last great cause', above all things, was its satisfying emotional simplicity. But it also perpetuated a category error that wrongly equates simplicity with moral virtue. The case for the Second Spanish Republic having constituted a political and cultural project that was ethically superior to the one represented by Francoism does not in the least depend on arguing for the 'simplicity' of the cause, still less for its perfection.

The international volunteers who fought to save Spain's Republican democracy were men and women of their times. And as times go, the 1930s and early 1940s were more difficult, painful, and 'imperfect' than most. Very many brigaders fought more than one war, as Republican Spaniards did – all the while without the easy certainties of patriotism or even the minimal security of a homeland. In that too they epitomized their times. For the Civil War of mid-20th century Europe saw all countries and all nations explode; 1939–45 was the bloody endgame of years of internecine conflict – social and cultural as well as political. No neat national categories obtained. It was a war fought over the brutal categorization at the heart of the Nazi new order in which resisters, bystanders, and collaborators were to be found in virtually all countries on the European continent. That popular memory did not for many subsequent decades (and in some cases still does not) 'remember' it this way indicates just how successfully that past was reconfigured in accordance with post-war political needs – doubtless themselves reinforced by an overwhelming desire among exhausted, war-torn populations to forget. But if we look at the history of those times rather than the memory of them, then it is surely unreasonable and unfair that the spurious argument of 'Spain' not having been a belligerent 'nation' in the Second World War should still be invoked to debar Spanish Republican veterans of the D-Day landings from participating in the commemorations – as they were debarred from those of 2004, the last in which there will be a living link with the events commemorated.

The past is another country. But doing history is, by definition, an unending dialogue between the present and the past. Much of what was at stake in Spain remains in present-day dilemmas at whose heart lie issues of race, religion, gender, and other forms of culture war that challenge us not to resort to political or other types of violence. In short, as this book's epigraph exhorts, we should not mythologize our fears and turn them as weapons on those who are different. The Spanish Civil War and all the other civil wars of Europe's mid-20th century were configured in great part by this mythologizing of fear, by a hatred of difference. The greatest challenge of the 21st century is, then, not to do this. It is an exhortation of particular relevance to Spain itself as, for the first time in its modern history, it becomes a country of inward migration. But it is no less apposite for other Europeans. For the space of the camp is still with us – sadly, not only as an historical memory. As the Hungarian poet Miklós Radnóti, who invoked Republican Spain and the friends who had died in combat there as symbols of what made the fight still worthwhile, wrote in July 1944, imprisoned in a German-controlled labour camp near Bor in Serbia and only months before he was himself killed by Hungarian guards on the prisoners' forced march in the wake of the retreating German army:

> Among false rumours and worms, we live here with Frenchmen, Poles,
> Loud Italians, heretic Serbs, nostalgic Jews, in the mountains.
> This feverish body, dismembered but still living one life, waits
> For good news, for women's sweet words, for a life both free and human,

Spain's Civil War, as a war of cultures, remains a parable for our times as much as it was for Radnóti's, as we search for that still elusive 'life both free and human'. The parable remains – even though the forms of our inhumanity to one another are each time differently configured.

References

Chapter 1

The epigraph, 'Long live those who bring us the rule of law', was the greeting offered in one village to republican campaigners shortly before the declaration of the Second Republic.

Under the terms of the Treaty of Cartagena (1907) the Great Powers had allotted Spain – which already controlled the North African enclaves of Ceuta and Melilla – the task of policing northern Morocco.

The text of the declaration broadcast by Franco from Spanish Morocco at the time of the military rising can be consulted in F. Díaz-Plaja, *La guerra de España en sus documentos* (Barcelona: Ediciones G. P., 1969), pp. 11–13.

Chapter 2

American journalist Jay Allen's interview with Franco in *The News Chronicle*, 29 July, 1 August 1936.

The quote from one of the Spanish journalists accompanying Franco's southern army is in M. Sánchez del Arco, *El sur de España en la reconquista de Madrid* (Seville: Editorial Sevillana, 1937), p. 205.

Chapter 3

The hostility of the British elites to the Spanish Republic did not diminish across the Civil War. In 1938 one Foreign Office respondent described the Republican Minister of Justice, the socialist member of parliament and miners' leader Ramón González Peña as 'a tinker from [Asturias]' (W 13853/29/41, F. O. General Correspondence: Spain, Public Records Office).

The caption on the famous Republican literacy poster reads: 'Illiteracy blinds the spirit. Soldier, educate yourself.' The poster is reproduced in H. Graham and J. Labanyi (eds) *Spanish Cultural Studies. An Introduction* (Oxford: Oxford University Press, 1995), p. 158.

Chapter 5

The most recent study of how the Republic managed to arm itself is Gerald Howson's *Arms for Spain* (London: John Murray, 1998). Scholarly disagreements are still too numerous for us to speak of a consensus on why the Republic lost the Civil War. But given the empirical evidence, few specialists would seek to argue that the Republic was on an equal footing with the Francoist camp in terms of quantity or quality of military aid received. For the most up-to-date calculations of Soviet aid, see G. Howson, *Arms for Spain*, Appendix 3, pp. 278–303, and especially the summary of material on pp. 302–3.

Chapter 6

The quote describing the Murzak action is from J. Cercas, *Soldados de Salamina* (Barcelona: Tusquets Editores, 2001), p. 158 (translation mine); English translation, *Soldiers of Salamis* (London: Bloomsbury, 2003).

The child who experienced both a Nazi concentration camp and a Francoist reformatory was Michel de Castillo, *Tanguy, Histoire d'un enfant d'aujourd'hui* (Paris: Gallimard, 1957) (English translation, *A Child of Our Time* (Alfred A. Knopf, 1956)).

The CEDA supporter who commented on the absence of freedom in Franco's Spain was Petra Román de Bondia, interviewed for the final programme of the Granada television series *The Spanish Civil War*, produced in the early 1980s.

Chapter 7

On memory, loss, and our encounter with Europe's dark mid-20th-century history, see W. G. Sebald, *The Emigrants* (London: The Harvill Press, 1996). On historical recuperation as an act of solidarity with the dead, see Patrick Modiano, *Dora Bruder* (Berkeley/Los Angeles: University of California Press, 1999) (original French, Paris: Editions Gallimard, 1997). The quote is from the American edition, p. 81.

The story of Bill Aalto is given in Helen Graham, 'Fighting the war, breaking the mould: Bill Aalto (1915–1958)', in R. Baxell, H. Graham, and P. Preston (eds), *More than One Kind of Fight: New Histories of the International Brigades in Spain* (London: Routledge/Cañada Blanch, 2006). There is a basic outline of Aalto's life in P. Carroll, *The Odyssey of the Abraham Lincoln Brigade. Americans in the Spanish Civil War* (Stanford, Ca.: Stanford University Press, 1994), pp. 118, 167f., 254–8.

G. Agamben, 'The Camp as Biopolitical Paradigm of the Modern', *Homo Sacer. Sovereign Power and Bare Life* (Stanford, Ca.: Stanford University Press, 1998). See also A. Weiner, *Landscaping the Human Garden* (Stanford, Ca.: Stanford University Press, 2003).

Miklós Radnóti, 'Seventh Eclogue, Lager Heideman, in the mountains above Žagubica, July 1944 .

Further reading

Introductory texts

Primer and introductory texts in English on the Spanish Civil War include S. Ellwood, *The Spanish Civil War* (Oxford: Blackwell/Historical Association Studies, 1991); M. Blinkhorn, *Democracy and Civil War in Spain 1931-1939*, 2nd edn. (London: Routledge, 1992); A. Forrest, *The Spanish Civil War* (London: Routledge, 2000); F. Lannon, *The Spanish Civil War* (Oxford: Osprey Essential Histories, 2002); and P. Preston, *A Concise History of the Spanish Civil War* (London: Fontana, 1996).

Bibliographies

Those looking for a bibliographical essay on the Spanish Civil War can consult the one in Paul Preston's *A Concise History of the Spanish Civil War*, or his introduction, 'War of Words' in P. Preston (ed.), *Revolution and War in Spain 1931-1939* (London: Routledge, 1995). There is also a briefer bibliographical note in Michael Alpert, *A New International History of the Spanish Civil War*, 2nd edn. (Basingstoke: Macmillan Palgrave, 2003). No detailed military history exists in English, but the essay by Preston surveys the available material. See also M. Alpert, 'The Clash of Spanish Armies: Contrasting Ways of War in Spain 1936–1939', *War in History*, 6: 3 (1999).

Background

For a discussion of the context of purificatory, genocidal, and retributive conflicts in 1920s, 1930s, and 1940s Europe, see Mark Mazower, *Dark Continent: Europe's Twentieth Century* (Harmondsworth: Penguin, 1998); J. Casanova, 'Civil Wars, Revolutions and Counterrevolutions in Finland, Spain and Greece (1918–1949): A Comparative Analysis', *International Journal of Politics, Culture and Society*, vol. 13, no. 3 (2000); and István Deák, Jan T. Gross, and Tony Judt (eds), *The Politics of Retribution in Europe: World War II and its Aftermath* (Princeton: Princeton University Press, 2000).

Civil War histories, memoirs, and novels

M. Alpert, *A New International History of the Spanish Civil War*, 2nd edn. (Basingstoke: Macmillan Palgrave, 2003)

A. Barea, *The Forging of a Rebel* (autobiographical trilogy) (London: Fontana, 1984; first published 1946)

R. Baxell, *British Volunteers in the Spanish Civil War. The British Battalion in the International Brigades, 1936–1939* (London: Routledge/Cañada Blanch, 2004)

R. Baxell, H. Graham, and P. Preston (eds), *More than One Kind of Fight: New Histories of the International Brigades in Spain* (London: Routledge/Cañada Blanch, 2006)

F. Borkenau, *The Spanish Cockpit* (London: Pluto Press, 1986; first published 1937)

G. Brenan, *The Spanish Labyrinth* (Cambridge: Cambridge University Press, 1990; first published 1943)

R. Carr, *The Spanish Tragedy* (London: Weidenfeld and Nicolson, 1977; reprinted in 1986 as *The Civil War in Spain*)

P. N. Carroll, *The Odyssey of the Abraham Lincoln Brigade* (Stanford, Ca.: Stanford University Press, 1994)

J. Casanova, *Anarchism, the Republic and Civil War in Spain 1931–1939* (London: Routledge/Cañada Blanch Studies, 2005)

J. Cercas, *Soldiers of Salamis* (novel) (London: Bloomsbury, 2003); original, *Soldados de Salamina* (Barcelona: Tusquets Editores, 2001)

D. D. Collum (ed.), *African Americans in the Spanish Civil War: This ain't Ethiopia but it'll do* (New York: G. K. Hall, 1992)

C. Ealham, *Class, Culture and Conflict in Barcelona, 1898–1937* (London: Routledge/Cañada Blanch, 2004)

R. Fraser, *Blood of Spain: The Experience of Civil War, 1936–39*, 3rd edn. (London: Penguin Books, 1988)

H. Graham, *The Spanish Republic at War 1936–39* (Cambridge: Cambridge University Press, 2002)

H. Graham, 'Spain's Memory Wars', *History Today*, May 2004

H. Graham and J. Labanyi (eds), *Spanish Cultural Studies: An Introduction* (Oxford: Oxford University Press, 1995), especially Part II and Part III

G. Harrison, *Night Train to Granada: From Sydney's Bohemia to Franco's Spain – An Offbeat Memoir* (Annandale, New South Wales, Australia: Pluto Press, 2002)

G. Howson, *The Flamencos of Cadiz Bay*, 2nd edn. (Westport, CT: The Bold Strummer, 1994; first published 1965)

G. Howson, *Arms for Spain* (London: John Murray, 1998)

A. Jackson, *British Women and the Spanish Civil War* (London: Routledge/Cañada Blanch, 2002)

F. Lannon, *Privilege, Persecution and Prophecy: The Catholic Church in Spain, 1875–1975* (Oxford: Clarendon Press, 1987)

C. Leitz and D. J. Dunthorn (eds), *Spain in an International Context 1936–1959* (Oxford/New York: Berghahn Books, 1999)

M. Low and J. Breá, *Red Spanish Notebook* (San Francisco: City Lights Books, 1979; first published 1937)

E. Moradiellos, 'British Political Strategy in the Face of the Military Rising of 1936 in Spain', *Contemporary European History*, I, 2 (1992)

E. Moradiellos, 'Appeasement and Non-Intervention: British Policy during the Spanish Civil War', in P. Catterall and C. J. Morris (eds), *Britain and the Threat to Stability in Europe 1918–45* (Leicester: Leicester University Press, 1993)

D. W. Pike, *Spaniards in the Holocaust: Mauthausen, the Horror on the Danube* (London: Routledge/Cañada Blanch, 2000)

P. Preston, *Franco* (London: Harper Collins, 1993)

P. Preston, *A Concise History of the Spanish Civil War* (London: Fontana, 1996)

P. Preston, *¡Comrades! Portraits from the Spanish Civil War* (London: Harper Collins, 1999)

P. Preston, 'The Great Civil War 1914–1945', in T. C. W. Blanning (ed.), *The Oxford History of Modern Europe* (Oxford: Oxford University Press, 2000)

P. Preston, *Doves of War: Four Women of Spain* (London: Harper Collins, 2002)

P. Preston (ed.) *Revolution and War in Spain 1931–1939* (London: Routledge, 1995; first published 1984)

P. Preston and A. Mackenzie (eds) *The Republic Besieged: Civil War in Spain 1936–1939* (Edinburgh: Edinburgh University Press, 1996)

H. Raguer, *The Catholic Church and the Spanish Civil War* (London: Routledge/Cañada Blanch Studies, forthcoming 2006)

M. Richards, *A Time of Silence: Civil War and the Culture of Repression in Franco's Spain, 1936–1945* (Cambridge: Cambridge University Press, 1998)

J. Semprún, *Literature or Life* (London: Viking (Penguin), 1997); original, *L'ecriture ou la vie* (Paris: Editions Gallimard, 1994)

R. Sender Barayón, *A Death in Zamora* (Albuquerque: University of New Mexico Press, 1989; 2nd edn., Calm Unity Press, 2003)

L. Stein, *Beyond Death and Exile: The Spanish Republicans in France, 1939–1955* (Cambridge, Mass.: Harvard University Press, 1979)

H. Thomas, *The Spanish Civil War* (Harmondsworth: Penguin, 1977)

Gamel Woolsey, *Death's Other Kingdom* (London: Longmans, Green and Co., 1939)

Websites

1. GCE list, created in 1996; the main Spanish Civil War website (predominantly in Spanish):
   www.guerracivil.org

2. Amigos de las Brigadas Internacionales (Spain):
   www.brigadasinternacionales.org

3. 'For Your Liberty and Ours': multimedia educational programmes produced by the Abraham Lincoln Brigade Archives; Series Editor, Fraser M. Ottanelli (material predominantly in English):
   www.alba-valb.org (ALBA website)

(i) Jewish volunteers in the Spanish Civil War:
www.alba-valb.org/curriculum/index.php?module=1

(ii) African Americans in the Spanish Civil War:
www.alba-valb.org/curriculum/index.php?module=2

(iii) Children's art during the Spanish Civil War ('They Still Draw Pictures: Teaching Materials'):
www.alba-valb.org/curriculum/index.php?module=3

(iv) Teaching the Spanish Civil War: tools for teachers and educators:
www.alba-valb.org/curriculum/index.php?module=4

(v) a brief bibliography on the history of the Abraham Lincoln Brigade at:
www.nyu.edu/library/bobst/research/tam/collections.html#alba

4. Website of the Asociación para la Recuperación de la Memoria Histórica (Association for the Recuperation of Historical Memory) which has spearheaded the campaign to open Spain's mass war graves and identify those buried there (text in Spanish):
www.memoriahistorica.org

5. International Brigade Memorial Trust.
www.international-brigades.org.uk

Chronology

1936

July

17–18   Military rebellion begins in Spanish North Africa and spreads to garrisons in mainland Spain.

18–20   Rebellion defeated in Madrid and Barcelona.

24–25   French cabinet headed by parliamentary socialist Léon Blum stalls on its initial offer of military aid to the Spanish Republic.

28   Hitler and Mussolini each decide independently to aid military rebels. First planes arrive in Morocco to airlift the Army of Africa (commanded by Franco) to mainland Spain (Seville).

August

Army of Africa fans out from Seville and begins its bloody march up through the south towards Madrid.

2   France announces its adherence to a policy of Non-Intervention.

14   Mass killings at Badajoz (Extremadura) after Franco's troops take the town.

15   British government bans the export of arms to Spain.

18   Federico García Lorca executed in Granada.

22   Madrid's Modelo prison is assaulted and political prisoners shot.

24   Soviet Union's first ambassador to Spain arrives in Madrid.

27–28   Aerial bombardment of Madrid begins.

September

3   Army of Africa takes Talavera, the last major centre on the southern advance to Madrid.

9   First meeting of Non-Intervention Committee in London.

18   Comintern executive agrees solidarity measures in support of the Spanish Republic, including recruitment of international volunteers to fight.

24   Anarcho-syndicalist CNT joins Catalan regional government.

25   Rebels issue decree forbidding political and trade union activity.

28   Franco's forces detour to Toledo, south-west of Madrid, to relieve garrison siege.

29   Soviet Union agrees to send arms to the Spanish Republic. Military junta appoints Franco to supreme political and military command of rebel zone.

30   Plá y Deniel, Bishop of Salamanca, issues a pastoral letter (entitled 'The Two Cities') defending the military rebels and in which, for the first time, the word 'crusade' is used to describe the Civil War. Republican government issues a decree signalling its intent to replace militia forces with a Popular Army subject to military discipline.

October

International Brigade volunteers begin to arrive.

1   Basque autonomy approved by Republican parliament.

7   Formation of autonomous Basque government under PNV leadership.

11   Amparo Barayón executed in Zamora.

November

6   Republican government moves to Valencia.

7   Battle for Madrid commences.

16   To assist Franco, Hitler dispatches Condor Legion, a special force equipped with latest German bomber and fighter aircraft and tanks.

18   Germany and Italy recognize Franco.

December

6 Mussolini agrees dispatch of an expeditionary force, Corpo di Truppe Volontarie (CTV), to assist Franco.

29 Pilar Espinosa executed in Candeleda (Avila).

1937

January

Mussolini massively increases supply of arms and troops to Franco.

2 British government makes 'gentleman's agreement' with Italy to maintain status quo in Mediterranean.

6 US establishes legal embargo on export of arms to Spain.

February

6–27 Battle of Jarama, on south-east Madrid front. First time in combat for the Abraham Lincoln Brigade. Republican forces, with Russian tank and air support, stem the rebel offensive which threatened to cut the Madrid–Valencia highway.

7 Málaga taken by rebels, with Italian assistance. Refugees fleeing towards Almería are heavily bombed.

March

8–18 Battle of Guadalajara on north-east Madrid front. Mussolini's troops sustain first defeat after meeting in combat other Italians – Internationals from the Garibaldi Brigade. The stalemate around Madrid continues for the rest of the war.

30 General Mola begins rebel offensive on northern front (Vizcaya) and German Condor Legion bombs Durango.

April

19 Franco decrees unification of Falange and Carlists in a single party under his leadership. Establishment of short-lived Non-Intervention Committee sea patrol.

26 Basque capital of Guernica destroyed by German and Italian saturation bombing.

May

3–7   Street fighting and popular protests in Barcelona (the 'May Days').

17   Parliamentary socialist Juan Negrín becomes prime minister of a new Republican cabinet.

31   Germany and Italy withdraw from Non-Intervention Committee sea patrol.

June

3   Death of General Mola in aircrash.

16   Arrest of POUM leaders in Barcelona.

19   Bilbao falls to Franco's troops.

21   Blum cabinet resigns in France.

30   Portugal withdraws from Non-Intervention sea patrol agreement.

July

1   Collective letter from Spanish bishops endorses Franco regime.

6–26   Battle of Brunete on western Madrid front.

August

Private religious ceremonies permitted once again in Republican Spain.
Franco implements naval blockade of Republic's Mediterranean ports.

24   Republican military offensive on north-eastern (Aragon) front. Attacks from unknown sources begin on neutral ships making for Spanish Republican ports.

26   Franco's troops take Santander.

September

10   Nyon Conference of main European powers convenes to discuss attacks by 'unknown' submarines on neutral shipping in the Mediterranean. Italy, widely known to be responsible, and Germany do not attend.

October

21   Fall of Republican North (Gijón and Avilés).

29   Republican government moves from Valencia to Barcelona.

November

6   Italy joins German-Japanese Anti-Comintern pact.

December

Air raids on Barcelona.

15   Republican forces commence Teruel offensive (Aragon).

24   Franco begins counter-offensive on Teruel front.

1938

January

7   Republican forces take town of Teruel.

February

22   Franco's forces re-take Teruel.

March

10   Franco launches new offensive in Aragon aiming to reach Mediterranean coast and cut Republican zone in two.

12   Franco repeals Republic's civil marriage law. Hitler occupies Austria.

13   Blum forms a new cabinet in France, and Negrín flies to Paris to plead for re-opening of French border.

16–18 Round the clock bombing of Barcelona by Italian planes based in Majorca.

17   French government opens border with Spain.

April

3   Franco's forces take Lérida.

8   Blum government falls in France and is replaced by a more conservative administration under Edouard Daladier.

15   Franco's forces reach the Mediterranean at Vinaroz and split the Republic in two.

16   Anglo-Italian Agreement. This was commonly understood in international diplomatic circles to signal Britain's implicit acceptance that Italian troops would remain in Spain until the end of the Civil War.

21   Franco begins offensive against Valencia.

May

1	Negrín publishes Republic's 13-point programme of war aims.
4	Vatican agrees full diplomatic relations with Franco.
11	Spanish Republic unsuccessfully petitions League of Nations for an end to Non-Intervention.
23	Republican army's XIV (guerrilla) corps carries out an innovative commando raid, liberating Republican soldiers imprisoned in the coastal fortress of Carchuna (Motril, Granada) just behind rebel lines.
24	First papal nuncio formally received by Franco.

June

13	French government closes border with Spain.

July

5	Non-Intervention Committee approves plan to withdraw international volunteers from Spain.
25	Republican army launches the Ebro offensive, the greatest battle of the war; its aim is to relieve Franco's military pressure on Valencia, but also to turn the international diplomatic tide.

August

17	Negrín militarizes Catalan arms factories in order to impose central government control. Catalan and Basque ministers resign from his cabinet in protest.
18	Franco refuses all peace initiatives.

September

29	Munich conference between Britain, France, Germany, and Italy. France and Britain agree to Hitler's annexation of Czech Sudetenland.

October

Battle of the Ebro continues.

4	Republic withdraws foreign volunteers from line in accordance with Non-Intervention Committee plan.

8	With tacit support of the Vatican, Negrín creates a commission to oversee the re-introduction of public worship in Catalonia.
24	Trial of POUM leaders begins.
29	Farewell parade of International Brigades in Barcelona.

November

| 16 | Battle of the Ebro ends as Republican forces retreat back across the river. More than a military defeat, the Ebro was a political defeat determined by the outcome at Munich. |
| 29 | Air attacks on Barcelona and Valencia. |

December

| 19 | Germany takes control of various Spanish mining operations. |
| 23 | Franco begins his offensive against Catalonia. |

1939

January

| 23 | Negrín declares martial law in Republican zone. |
| 26 | Franco's troops take Barcelona. Mass flight of refugees to French frontier. |

February

1	Republican parliament meets for the last time on Spanish soil at the castle of Figueres.
9	Franco issues the Law of Political Responsibilities which retrospectively redefines Republican political activity as criminal.
10	Fall of Catalonia. Franco closes frontier with France. Negrín flies back to Republican centre-south zone.
27	Britain and France recognize Franco.

March

| 4–6 | Confused revolt at Republican naval base in Cartagena results in fleet setting sail. It is interned by the French in North Africa, pending delivery to Franco. The Republic thus loses the means of evacuating thousands of refugees who fear for their lives. |

5   Colonel Segismundo Casado, Republican commander on the
       Madrid front, rebels against Negrín in the mistaken belief that,
       as an army officer, he will be able to negotiate with Franco a
       'peace with guarantees'.

6–13   Street fighting in Madrid between pro- and anti-Casado forces.
       Republican army elsewhere in centre-south zone holds aloof.

26–28 Casado's forces win in Madrid, but Franco refuses to negotiate.
       Casado has no choice but to order the Republican air force and
       army to surrender.

27   Franco's troops occupy Madrid. Mass flight of refugees;
       Republican refugees congregate in the Mediterranean ports,
       especially Alicante, but relatively few escape due to lack of
       boats. Franco signs the Anti-Comintern pact.

April

1   Franco issues his final war communiqué announcing the end of
       military hostilities. The USA recognizes Franco's regime.

6   Franco makes public Spain's adherence to the Anti-Comintern
       pact.

Glossary

CEDA (Spanish Confederation of Right Wing Groups): nationwide mass Catholic party formed in 1933 and heavily reliant on the Church's organizational networks.

CNT (National Confederation of Labour): anarcho-syndicalist labour union founded in 1910.

Comintern: the Communist (or Third) International, established by Lenin in 1919 to be an organization of all national communist parties.

Falange: Spanish fascist party founded in 1933 by José Antonio Primo de Rivera, whose father had been military dictator of Spain from 1923 to 1930.

PCE: the official Spanish communist party, founded in 1921 and affiliated to the Communist International (*Comintern*).

PNV: Basque nationalist party founded in 1895. The PNV was strongly Catholic and socially conservative, but it opposed the ultra-centralism of the Spanish Right.

POUM: dissident (i.e. non-*Comintern*-aligned) communist party formed in September 1935. The POUM was overwhelmingly a Catalan-based party.

PSOE: Spanish socialist party, founded in 1879.

Republican(s): denotes all those individuals and groups who supported the Republic during the Civil War of 1936–9.

republican(s): denotes members of parties and groups who were specifically republican in ideology.

UGT (Amalgamated Union of Workers): socialist-led trade union founded in 1888, traditionally strongest in Madrid and in the industrial zones of northern Spain, such as the Asturian coal mines and heavy industry of Vizcaya (Basque Country).

Index

A

Aalto, Bill 53, 101, 148, 153
Agriculture 3, 4, 5, 25
 counter-reform of 32
 reform of 7, 12, 137
airpower 42, 80, 96, 109, 110
Alfonso XIII 6
Alicante 113, 166
Allen, Jay 33
Almodóvar, Pedro 141
Alonso, Celestino 124
American Medical Bureau 46
Anarcho-syndicalists xii, 5, 6,
 13, 26, 64, 67, 72, 160, 167
Andalusia 32
Anticlericalism 5, 27, 82
Anti-Comintern pact 85, 163,
 166
Aragon 25, 63, 91, 93, 96, 97,
 101, 105, 107, 162, 163
Armaments, Republican
 procurement of 89–91, 99,
 152
Army xi, 1, 2, 3, 6, 7–8, 9, 10,
 16, 18, 19, 21, 33, 91
 post civil-war 75–6, 129
 rebel/Francoist zone 23–4,
 30–1, 32, 33, 51, 68, 69, 71,
 73–4, 79, 80, 96, 159
 Republican zone 48, 52, 53,
 79, 91–94, 100, 107, 109,
 110, 112, 113, 147, 160, 166
 Republican army and
 guerrilla warfare 53, 55,
 100–1, 122, 164

Association for the
 Recuperation of
 Historical Memory
 (ARMH) 141–2, 146
Asturias 16, 59, 168
Austria (*Anschluss*) 96, 98, 99,
 113, 162
Auxilio Social 77
Avilés 93, 162

B

Badajoz 33, 159
Bancic, Olga 123
Barayón, Amparo xiii, 29, 30,
 132, 142–3, 160
Barbieri, Francesco 66
Barcelona 5, 6, 25, 51, 63, 64,
 65, 66, 96, 98, 101, 102,
 127, 159, 162, 163, 165
Basque Country 10, 11, 23,
 52–3, 71, 82, 91, 102, 132,
 160, 164, 168
Basque nationalist party
 (PNV) 52, 160, 167
Belchite 93, 121
Belgium 71
Berlanga, Luis 61
Berneri, Camillo 66
Bilbao 67, 162
Biopolitics 84, 153
Blitzkrieg 96, 110
Blockade of Republican ports
 91, 95, 99, 101, 105–6, 162
Blue Division 75, 125
Blum, Léon 39, 159, 162, 163
Boix, Francisco 127, 128, 129
Bombing ix, 26, 49, 71–3, 96,
 120, 159, 161,163

Botwin, Naftali 44
Britain 33, 35, 37, 38–9, 40,
    41, 67, 71, 81, 87, 88–9, 95,
    96, 98, 99, 109, 110,
    113–14, 121, 151–2, 159,
    161,163, 164, 165
Brunete, battle of 53, 121, 162
Buchenwald 126

C

Cabanellas, General Miguel 70
Cantalupo, Roberto 73
Carchuna (Motril) 100, 164
Carlists 11, 24, 75, 161
Cartagena 89, 113, 165
Casado, Colonel Segismundo
    166
Català, Neus 119
Catalonia 2, 4, 10, 22, 63, 64,
    65, 96, 98, 101–2, 104,
    105–6, 111, 115, 132, 144,
    145, 160, 164, 165
Catholic Church 2, 4–5, 6, 7,
    8–9, 10, 11, 12, 27, 33, 34,
    75, 82–3, 85, 86, 103–4,
    134–5, 145, 162, 167
Catholicism 2, 4–5, 10–11, 12,
    14, 22, 23, 28–9, 68, 85,
    131, 133, 135
Causa General 133, 141
Cercas, Javier 115, 122, 146, 152
Checas 65
Churchill, Winston 82
Cinema 78–9
Civil marriage law, repeal of
    163
Cold War 125
Communist International

(Comintern) 47, 48, 49,
    65, 67, 104, 105, 160, 167
Communists xii, 61, 64, 65, 67,
    89, 102, 104–5, 109, 112,
    119, 120, 167
Concentration camps 44, 75,
    115, 117, 118, 119, 121, 123,
    126, 127, 129, 131, 150,
    152, 153
Condor Legion 71, 160, 161
Constitutionalism 8, 12, 84,
    102–4, 107–8, 109
Cultural bolshevism 60
Czechoslovakia 110, 164

D

Daladier, Edouard 117, 163
Darwin, Charles 60
D-Day landings 149
De Gaulle, Charles 121
Denunciation 85, 86, 135, 140
Diplomacy xi, 67, 83, 94–5,
    98–9, 100, 101, 103–4,
    109, 110–111, 164
Divorce, reversal of 134
Durango 71, 161
Durruti, Buenaventura 50

E

Ebro, battle of 108–110, 121,
    123, 164, 165
Eden, Anthony 81
Education 7, 12, 14, 57, 132
Edwards,Thyra 46
Empire 2, 3, 73, 81, 83, 84, 133
Espinosa, Pilar 29, 141–2, 161
Espionage 66, 107–8, 113
Ethiopia 33

Extra-judicial killing 27,
    28–32, 35, 38, 74–5, 108,
    133, 137, 141
Extremadura 32, 159

F

Falange 24, 28, 29, 30, 61, 70,
    75, 76, 82, 83, 85, 125, 126,
    136, 161, 167
    Sección Femenina in 76–8,
    136
Fascism x, 1, 9, 19, 24, 44, 75,
    122, 139
Federalism 4
Figueres 165
Finnish civil war 43
First Republic 8
First World War x, 1, 5, 43
France 35, 37, 39, 40, 41, 66,
    67, 81, 91, 93, 95, 96, 98,
    99, 110, 113–14, 115, 117,
    119, 121, 122, 159, 163,
    164, 165
    French Communist Party
    (PCF) 47
    Revolution of 1789 7
    Spanish Republicans in
    Resistance 44, 117–118,
    120, 122–3, 124, 125
Franco, General Francisco xi,
    3, 9, 16, 32, 33, 34, 35, 38,
    40, 42, 51, 69–75, 81, 83,
    85, 87, 88, 89, 90, 91,
    92, 93, 95, 99, 100, 103,
    108, 113, 114, 115, 116,
    122, 125, 126, 133,
    141, 148, 160, 164,
    165, 166

war strategy 73–4, 79, 80,
    93–4, 96, 98, 109–10, 111,
    165
Franco, Nicolás 75
Franco, Ramón 70
Francoism xi, 83–6, 119,
    129–37, 138, 139,
    146
Freemasonry 82, 134, 138

G

Galicia 23
Gandía 113
García, Antonio 127
García Lorca, Federico 29, 159
Gender 2, 11–12, 29, 32, 46–7,
    53, 55–7, 61, 76, 119, 129,
    135, 147
Germany 33, 35, 36, 37, 38–9,
    41, 51, 68, 69, 71, 75, 79,
    80, 81, 82, 85, 87, 88, 90,
    95, 100, 106, 109, 110, 111,
    113–14, 120, 125, 127, 160,
    162, 164, 165
Gijón 93, 162
Goering, Hermann 113
Goff, Irv 53, 101, 148
Gold, Republican mobilization
    of 89, 99
Grzywacz, Shloime 124
Guadalajara, battle of 42, 80,
    121, 161
Guernica 71, 145, 161

H

Heartfield, John 58
History writing xi, 133, 138–41,
    147

Hitler, Adolf 1, 24, 38, 39, 48, 51, 69, 79, 81, 82, 114, 120, 122, 125, 141, 159, 160, 164

Hunger 105–7, 136

Hutchins, Evelyn 46

I

Ibárruri, Dolores 120

Industry 3, 4, 24, 25, 73, 168

International Brigades 42–6, 47–9, 79, 80, 99, 109–10, 117, 123, 139, 148–9, 160, 161, 164, 165

  African American brigaders 44–5

  Jewish brigaders 44

Italy 33, 35, 36, 37, 38–9, 41, 51, 68, 69, 71, 75, 79, 80, 81, 85, 87, 88, 90, 95, 96, 100, 106, 110, 113–14, 160, 161, 162, 163, 164

J

Japan 37, 85

Jarama, battle of 42, 45, 80, 145, 161

K

Kea, Salaria 46

Kerensky, Alexander 38

Komsomol 90

L

Landa, Matilde 129–30

'Last great cause' 147–8

Law, Oliver xiii, 45

Law of Political Responsibilities 111, 134, 165

League of Nations 98, 164

Leclerc, General Philippe 121, 123

Lenin, Vladimir Ilich 167

Lerida (Lleida) 96, 163

Literacy 56, 57, 60, 152

M

Madrid 24, 25, 32, 35, 40, 42, 49, 51, 52, 53, 61, 71, 72, 80, 89, 91, 93, 95, 112, 121, 125, 159, 160, 166, 168

Maes, Magdalena 132

Malaga 25, 51, 161

Mannerheim, Carl Gustav Emil, Baron von 43

Maquis 119, 120

Marshall Plan 136

Martial law 134, 165

Mauthausen 126, 127

'May Days' (Barcelona 1937) 63–7, 101, 102, 162

McCarthy, Joseph 148

Medical advances 46

Memory 127, 137, 141, 143–4, 146–7, 149, 153

Mexico 89, 115

Migration 137

Miliciana 55, 56

Moa, Pío 146, 147

Mobilization x, 11, 22, 61, 76, 147

  rebel/Francoist zone 76, 77–8, 85

Republican zone 24, 36, 37, 53–8, 59
Modiano, Patrick 144, 153
Mola, General Emilio 33, 35, 69, 73, 161, 162
Monarchy 4, 6, 7
Morales, Diego 126
Morocco 9, 33, 151, 159
Munich agreement 110–111, 112, 113, 164, 165
Mussolini, Benito 1, 24, 38, 39, 48, 51, 66, 69, 75, 79, 113, 159, 161

N

Nacht und Nebel 126
Narvik (Norway) 121
Nazism xi, 1, 44, 60, 82, 85, 86, 125
  new order in Europe 81, 85, 114, 119, 120, 121, 122, 129, 149, 150
Negrín, Juan 63, 67, 87, 94–95, 98, 99, 100–4, 105, 108, 111–112, 113, 136, 162, 163, 164, 165
Nelken, Margarita 120–1
Nin, Andreu 65–6
Non-Intervention 37, 40, 41, 49, 68, 81, 82, 87–91, 93, 94, 98, 99, 101, 105, 111, 159, 160, 161, 162, 163, 164
Nuremberg 127
Nyon Conference 162

O

Orwell, George 64, 65
OVRA 66

P

Pasionaria *see* Ibárruri, Dolores
Plá y Deniel, Bishop of Salamanca 160
Pointner, Anna 127
Poland 89
Political prisoners 84, 129, 130, 131–2
  children in prison/ reformatories 130–1, 143
Popular Party (PP) 144
Population 4
Portugal 88, 162
POUM 65–7, 108–9, 162, 165, 167
Prieto, Indalecio 101, 104
Primo de Rivera, General Miguel 6, 8
Primo de Rivera, José Antonio 9, 74, 167
Propaganda 58, 59, 60, 72
Purges 132

Q

Queipo de Llano, General Gonzalo 22

R

Racism 34, 44–5, 82
Radnóti, Miklós 150
Ravensbrück 119, 126
Refugees x, 35, 51, 64, 71, 105, 117, 118, 120, 161, 165, 166
Regenerationism 60
Renau, Josep 58

Index

Republican identities 49–50, 57–8, 73, 85, 92–3, 147

Republicans xii, 35, 75, 101, 117, 118, 119, 132, 136, 137, 167

in Second World War 120–7, 149

republicans xii, 6, 7, 10, 14, 17, 89, 102, 167

Revolution 24–8, 36, 147

curtailment of 63, 103

Rivas, Manuel 23

Rojo, General Vicente 91–2, 94

Rol-Tanguy, Henri 123

Rolfe, Edwin 45–6

Rosselli, Carlo 66

Rosselli, Nello 66

Russian revolution 1, 5, 38

and civil war 66

S

Salamanca 70, 83, 144, 145

Sanjurjo, General, José 103

Sebald, W.G. 153

Second World War ix, xi, 45, 46, 51, 53, 75, 109, 111, 117–27, 136, 149, 150

Semprún, Jorge 126–7, 131

Sender, Ramón J. 29

Serrano Suñer, Ramón 74–5, 126

Seville 3, 22, 159

Silva, Emilio 142

Social Darwinism 18, 60

Socialists xii, 7, 8, 10, 13, 14, 16, 17, 67, 89, 95, 102, 104, 167, 168

Soviet Union 40–1, 47, 61–63, 66, 71, 79, 88, 89, 90, 92, 99–100, 110, 111, 112, 120–1, 159, 160, 161

Spengler, Oswald 9, 122

Stalags 117, 126

Stalin, Josef 26, 40–1, 48, 99

Stalingrad 120

T

Talavera de la Reina 35, 160

Taussig, Michael 146–7

Teruel 93–94, 95, 96, 101, 163

Toledo 34, 40, 70, 160

Transition to democracy 139, 140, 141

Trotsky, Leon 65

U

Unamuno, Miguel de 68, 83

Unemployment 14, 43, 64

United Nations 142

United States 45, 63, 136, 161, 166

V

Valencia 4, 22, 26, 50, 51, 58, 98, 106, 109, 110, 113, 160, 162, 164, 165

Valley of the Fallen 131

Vatican 82, 83, 104, 164, 165

Vigo 23

Vinaroz 96, 98, 163

W

Wolf, Francisc 124

Women *see* gender

Woolsey, Gamel 25

Work 131–2, 133

Y

Youth 2, 11, 15–16, 54, 61, 127, 147

Z

Zaragoza 3, 9

Expand your collection of
VERY SHORT INTRODUCTIONS

1. Classics
2. Music
3. Buddhism
4. Literary Theory
5. Hinduism
6. Psychology
7. Islam
8. Politics
9. Theology
10. Archaeology
11. Judaism
12. Sociology
13. The Koran
14. The Bible
15. Social and Cultural Anthropology
16. History
17. Roman Britain
18. The Anglo-Saxon Age
19. Medieval Britain
20. The Tudors
21. Stuart Britain
22. Eighteenth-Century Britain
23. Nineteenth-Century Britain
24. Twentieth-Century Britain
25. Heidegger
26. Ancient Philosophy
27. Socrates
28. Marx
29. Logic
30. Descartes
31. Machiavelli
32. Aristotle
33. Hume
34. Nietzsche
35. Darwin
36. The European Union
37. Gandhi
38. Augustine
39. Intelligence
40. Jung
41. Buddha
42. Paul
43. Continental Philosophy
44. Galileo
45. Freud
46. Wittgenstein
47. Indian Philosophy
48. Rousseau
49. Hegel
50. Kant
51. Cosmology
52. Drugs
53. Russian Literature
54. The French Revolution
55. Philosophy
56. Barthes
57. Animal Rights
58. Kierkegaard
59. Russell
60. Shakespeare
61. Clausewitz
62. Schopenhauer
63. The Russian Revolution
64. Hobbes
65. World Music
66. Mathematics
67. Philosophy of Science
68. Cryptography
69. Quantum Theory
70. Spinoza

71. Choice Theory
72. Architecture
73. Poststructuralism
74. Postmodernism
75. Democracy
76. Empire
77. Fascism
78. Terrorism
79. Plato
80. Ethics
81. Emotion
82. Northern Ireland
83. Art Theory
84. Locke
85. Modern Ireland
86. Globalization
87. Cold War
88. The History of Astronomy
89. Schizophrenia
90. The Earth
91. Engels
92. British Politics
93. Linguistics
94. The Celts
95. Ideology

96. Prehistory
97. Political Philosophy
98. Postcolonialism
99. Atheism
100. Evolution
101. Molecules
102. Art History
103. Presocratic Philosophy
104. The Elements
105. Dada and Surrealism
106. Egyptian Myth
107. Christian Art
108. Capitalism
109. Particle Physics
110. Free Will
111. Myth
112. Hieroglyphs
113. Ancient Egypt
114. Medical Ethics
115. Kafka
116. Anarchism
117. Ancient Warfare
118. Global Warming
119. Christianity

Visit the
VERY SHORT
INTRODUCTIONS
Web site

www.oup.co.uk/vsi

➤ **Information** about all published titles

➤ News of **forthcoming books**

➤ **Extracts** from the books, including titles not yet published

➤ **Reviews** and views

➤ **Links** to other **web sites** and main OUP web page

➤ Information about **VSIs in translation**

➤ **Contact** the editors

➤ **Order** other **VSIs** on-line